CHRISTIAN CORE VALUES

FAMILY BIBLE STUDIES

DR. BRUCE CALDWELL

Copyright © 2021 by Dr. Bruce Caldwell

ISBN   Softcover   978-1-953537-88-1

All rights reserved. No part of this book may be reproduced or transmitted in any form or by any means, electronic or mechanical, including photocopying, recording, or by any information storage and retrieval system without express written permission from the author, except in the case of brief quotations embodied in critical reviews and certain other non-commercial uses permitted by copyright law.

Printed in the United States of America.

To order additional copies of this book, contact:
Bookwhip
1-855-339-3589
https://www.bookwhip.com

CONTENTS

Core Values for Christian Families 1

Core Value 01: Why Does the Bible Make Such a Big Deal About "Flattery" Being Wrong? 3
Core Value 02: What is that Aroma? 6
Core Value 03: What I Am Doing Just Feels Wrong 9
Core Value 04: Jesus Wept. Why? 12
Core Value 05: Grace, Faith and Works…in that Order 15
Core Value 06: I Am so Proud of You! 18
Core Value 07: The Trust and Faith of a Child 21
Core Value 08: What is the Big Deal About Reading the Bible? 24
Core Value 09: Who is in Charge Around Here: God or Satan? ...27
Core Value 10: Water Baptism is Good; Baptism by the Holy Spirit is Essential 30
Core Value 11: Should Genuine "Caring" for Someone Precede Witnessing to Them? 33
Core Value 12: But You Promised… ! 36
Core Value 13: The Devil Made Me Do It! 39
Core Value 14: Witnessing is Risky and Necessary! 42
Core Value 15: Fidelity, What is That? A Bank? 45
Core Value 16: Isn't Having Money a Good Thing? 48
Core Value 17: Who is Your Hero? Is There Someone You Really Want to be Like? 51
Core Value 18: How Can I Feel Joyful When My Life and the World Around Me Are Falling Apart? 54
Core Value 19: Who is Going to Explain the Scriptures to Me? ...57
Core Value 20: I Am Sooooo Mad! 60
Core Value 21: Finally, All this Stuff is Mine! 63
Core Value 22: Can a Fig Tree Yield Olives? 66
Core Value 23: When Did God Grieve Because of Me? 69

Core Value 24: Did I Choose God or Did He Choose Me?
Yes! and Yes!..72
Core Value 25: The Mystery of the Holy Spirit, Revealed 75
Core Value 26: When the Bible Speaks of "Blasphemy"
What Does that Mean?...78
Core Value 27: And the Greatest Commandment Is . . ? 81
Core Value 28: Are You a Foxhole Christian? 84
Core Value 29: A "Sippy Cup" Approach to Growth!....................87
Core Value 30: Got Too Much Stuff? Build a Bigger Barn!............ 90
Core Value 31: How Can You Possibly Speak as Jesus? 94
Core Value 32: Are Tattoos a Problem? 97
Core Value 33: One Very Bad Mark, 666, One Good Mark;
Choose!..100
Core Value 34: Whose Team Are You On? 103
Core Value 35: Does God Really Hear My Prayers? 106
Core Value 36: Did You Say "Ask Anything"?...............................109
Core Value 37: God Has No Grandchildren. 112
Core Value 38: Babel Reversed; A Pure Language Restored..........115
Core Value 39: Could Blessings Become Burdens?.......................118
Core Value 40: I Humbly Declare That I Out Ran All of You!......121
Core Value 41: Who Forgot to Water the Flowers?...................... 124
Core Value 42: Which Is It, Earthly Rewards or Eternal Rewards?...127
Core Value 43: I Know and You Don't! 130
Core Value 44: Unity in Jesus, Our Prayer....................................133
Core Value 45: Pull Together or be Pulled Apart..........................136
Core Value 46: Overcome or be Overcome...................................139
Core Value 47: To Be Forgiven Enables You to Forgive 142
Core Value 48: Perfected, Yet Not Perfect 145
Core Value 49: Isn't Being "Lukewarm" Better Than Being Cold?....148
Core Value 50: Last Here, First There, Disabled Here,
Enabled There...151
Core Value 51: My Church is Right. Your Church is Wrong!
Right?..154
Core Value 52: Hey Sailor!..157

CORE VALUES FOR CHRISTIAN FAMILIES

Many of us attend church, at least once in a while, and we sometimes read the Bible, but how can we be sure that our family is grounded in the fundamentals of Christianity? One way is to dedicate ourselves to a plan of study that involves the whole family. Why the whole family? Listen:

Deuteronomy 11:18-21 NKJV
...you shall lay up these words of mine in your heart and in your soul, and bind them as a sign on your hand, and they shall be as frontlets between your eyes. You shall teach them to your children, speaking of them when you sit in your house, when you walk by the way, when you lie down, and when you rise up. And you shall write them on the doorposts of your house and on your gates, that your days and the days of your children may be multiplied in the land of which the LORD swore to your fathers to give them, like the days of the heavens above the earth.

God, speaking through Moses, has commanded us to "teach His words" to our children. The task is far too important than to leave such teaching to others. One of the great advantages of learning God's word, as a family, is that assures you that your beliefs and understandings are "mutual."

I suspect that it is difficult, with all of the "agenda" that is coming at family members, to spend time together discussing the core values of Christianity. Yet, is anything more important? No, nothing is more important than knowing that every member of the family is seeking to do as Jesus commanded:

Matthew 22:37-39 NKJV
"'You shall love the LORD your God with all your heart, with all your soul, and with all your mind.' This is the first and great commandment. And the second is like it: 'You shall love your neighbor as yourself.'"

The purpose of these Family Bible Studies is to provide a format for getting each family member to discuss the scriptural topics at hand and to both learn and share mutual commitments. Since some of the concepts are more difficult to understand than others, fathers and mothers will have to assist in explaining what they mean and will, at times, need to restate the core value in words the children will understand.

These Studies are intentionally "substantive", that is, they will lead you into the meat of the word as opposed to dwelling on the milk of the word. Listen:

Hebrews 5:12-14 NKJV
For though by this time you ought to be teachers, you need some one to teach you again the first principles of God's word. You need milk, not solid food; for every one who lives on milk is unskilled in the word of righteousness, for he is a child. But solid food is for the mature, for those who have their faculties trained by practice to distinguish good from evil.

Establish a specific day and time for your Family Bible Study and be sure to begin the study with prayer. Draw near to God and He will draw near to you. May God abundantly bless your family as you learn "eternal" values. I pray that God will richly bless you and your family, forever.

CORE VALUE 01

WHY DOES THE BIBLE MAKE SUCH A BIG DEAL ABOUT "FLATTERY" BEING WRONG?

> **CORE CHRISTIAN VALUE**
>
> **Flattery is excessive and insincere praise intended to gain advantage. It is self serving and it is forbidden.**

What is flattery? The first entry for flattery in Webster's dictionary is: To praise excessively especially from motives of self-interest. Or to: To portray too favorably. Or to: to display to advantage. The basic truth is that flattery is an "over the top" statement generally offered in order to gain advantage for yourself. Have you ever seen someone telling a person how great they are, how wonderful they are, how awesome they are and every other superlative you can think of? A flatterer is one who says things to people and about people in order to gain advantage.

The question is; why do we offer flattering comments? For instance, if one kid says to another, "you are a totally righteous dude", do they really mean that or are they saying it so the other kid will like them, include them in their group and so on. No "dude" is totally righteous and that same dude could become your enemy or worse yet, use you to their own advantage. A genuine compliment of someone's talent is not flattery. It is an honest statement of sincere appreciation of their talent or accomplishments. We should not offer praise or compliments in order to "get something" in return. You may encourage someone and that may result in their liking you but if your motive is not "self-serving", you have done the right thing.

Listen to what Jude, the half brother of Jesus and the brother of James had to say about people who flatter: These are grumblers, complainers, walking according to their own lusts; and they mouth great swelling words, flattering people to gain advantage. "JUDE 1:16 NKJV. Jude's words match up perfectly with Webster's definition of flattery: Excessive praise, especially if you want to gain favor or advantage, is forbidden.

The Apostle Paul adds some information that is helpful. Listen: "For those who are such do not serve our Lord Jesus Christ, but their own belly, and by smooth words and flattering speech deceive the hearts of the simple." ROMANS 16:18 NKJV.

Paul taught you that in some cases, flattery and smooth words deceive the "simple". People who are "simple-minded" are easily deceived. You should see flattery for what it is; an attempt to manipulate and control you offered by a person who is seeking something from you. Don't you know when someone is "flattering" you? How does that make you feel?

What is an appropriate response to flattery? Should you immediately not trust that person? When you admire the qualities of a person, what sort of phrases can you use that will keep them from thinking that you are a "self-serving flatterer"?

For the "adults" in this study, listen to Solomon's words on this subject: "With her enticing speech she caused him to yield, with her flattering lips she seduced him." …a flattering mouth works ruin." PROVERBS 7:2, and 26:28 NKJV (men and women, please do not doubt this truth for one moment!).

NOTES/REFLECTIONS

CORE VALUE 02

WHAT IS THAT AROMA?

> **"CORE CHRISTIAN VALUE**
>
> We are to be imitators of Jesus Christ and in doing so we give off a sweet- smelling aroma, one that pleases God. That aroma may not please a person who does not love and honor God.

Have you ever considered the notion that you give off an aroma! We are not talking about whether you use deodorant or not. Listen to this quotation from the Bible:

"Now thanks be to God who always leads us in triumph in Christ, and through us diffuses the fragrance of His knowledge in every place. For we are to God the fragrance of Christ among those who are being saved and among those who are perishing. To the one we are the aroma of death leading to death, and to the other the aroma of life leading to life. And who is sufficient for these things? For we are not, as so many, peddling the word of God; but as of sincerity, but as from God, we speak in the sight of God in Christ." 2 CORINTHIANS 2:14-17 NKJV

Yes, we have a fragrance and if we love Jesus it is discernable, that is, people can tell that we love Jesus. The verses above teach us that the aroma of Jesus, in us, causes other Christians to notice that love but people whose hearts are far from God, also notice and they feel that we are a testimony, a witness, against their life style. The Christian might say that we are the aroma of life and the one who does not yet love Jesus might say, "What is that smell?" meaning you are making them uncomfortable.

The Bible says that it is God's will that no person perish, that is, to be banned from the presence of God forever. Therefore if someone is giving you a hard time because you have the aroma of Christ, it is not time to get into an argument with him or her. God loves them and is waiting patiently for them to repent, to turn from sin, and to have His Spirit and their spirit united. Our job is to love them even if they do not presently respect our love for Jesus.

Listen to one more quotation from the Apostle Paul: "Therefore be imitators of God as dear children. And walk in love, as Christ also has loved us and given Himself for us, an offering and a sacrifice to God for a sweet-smelling aroma." EPHESIANS 5:1-2 NKJV

We are that sweet smelling aroma that pleases God as we walk in love. God is love and to be like Jesus is our goal. No one is perfect, as Jesus was, but His Spirit in you gives you a chance to be an "imitator of God."

Discuss whether you think you give off a Christ-like aroma as you live your life. How do you feel about being criticized for trying to be like Jesus? What choices do you have in reacting to someone who thinks you are trying to be too "good"?

NOTES/REFLECTIONS

CORE VALUE 03

WHAT I AM DOING JUST FEELS WRONG

> **CORE CHRISTIAN VALUE**
>
> **Our lower nature (flesh) is at war with our spirit. We have a "built-in" knowledge of right and wrong. God wants to unite our spirit and His Spirit. He will strengthen us.**

The Apostle Paul presents a point of view you should consider. He says, "I don't understand myself at all, for I really want to do what is right, but I can't. I do what I don't want to-what I hate. I know perfectly well that what I am doing is wrong, and my bad conscience proves that I agree with these laws I am breaking. ROMANS 7:15-16 TLB

Paul is teaching us that we know what we should do and when we do bad things, we knew they were bad. He says our conscience proves to us that what we are doing is wrong.

Then Paul says: So you see how it is: my new life tells me to do right, but the old nature that is still inside me loves to sin. Oh, what a terrible predicament I'm in! Who will free me from my slavery to this deadly lower nature? Thank God! It has been done by Jesus Christ our Lord. He has set me free. ROMANS 7:23 TLB

What Paul describes as our "deadly lower nature", is the "default setting" we find ourselves in at birth. You know what a default setting is. For instance, if your new car measures the mileage as miles instead of kilometers, then the factory has preset the odometer to miles. You can take action to change the default setting to kilometers if you want to, but if you do not do so, it will continue to measure the distance you travel in miles.

If you find yourself wanting to change the default setting of your life from dominance by a deadly lower nature, often referred to as the dominance of the flesh, you must take action. You were born in the flesh but God placed in you, a spirit. God wants His Spirit and your spirit to be united, to be as one. When you agree that is what you want as well, you turn to Him ask him to forgive you for all the dumb things (sin) you have done. God promises that He will change the default setting of your heart from one of flesh to one of Spirit, His Spirit in you.

You will still have impulses to revert to your old default setting of "the flesh" but God has promised that he will intervene for you. Listen to His wonderful promise: No temptation has overtaken you except such as is common to man; but God is faithful, who will not allow you to be tempted beyond what you are able, but with the temptation will also make the way of escape, that you may be able to bear it. 1 CORINTHIANS 10:13 NKJV

How can you escape? First, understand that temptation does not come from God. When tempted, no one should say, "God is tempting me; "… for God cannot be tempted by evil, nor does he tempt anyone" JAMES 1:13 NIV. Who is the tempter? Remember when the comedian said "the devil made me do it". Does blaming the devil let you off the hook?

Can you defeat temptation by your own resolve? In this life will you ever be "not tempted"? Is victory over temptation ever "yours"? Know this: "God is my strength and power, and He makes my way perfect".

2 SAMUEL 22:33 NKJV

Do you sometimes feel like there is a tug of war going on inside you? How do you deal with it?

NOTES/REFLECTIONS

CORE VALUE 04

JESUS WEPT. WHY?

> **CORE CHRISTIAN VALUE**
>
> **We properly mourn over the death of a loved one but then we are encouraged, knowing that death is physical and not spiritual. Our spirits live on and a reunion of God's children awaits.**

The shortest verse in the Bible is, "Jesus wept", John 11:35. Yet that short verse reveals so much that we need to understand. The Apostle John saw Jesus weep when Mary and Martha, the sisters that Jesus knew well, told Him that Lazarus, their brother, had died.

First, we can see that Jesus had compassion upon those who loved Lazarus. That means that His heart ached when theirs did. He felt their loss, their pain, just as He feels our losses and pains. That is how much Jesus loves His children, His friends. When our hearts ache in circumstances of personal loss, such as the death or serious illness, of a loved one, Jesus feels our loss. We never have to go through such sadness alone.

Second, Jesus knew that He would call Lazarus forth from the grave in which he had laid dead for four days. He certainly did not weep because of the death of Lazarus. He wept because the friends and family of Lazarus were grieving. But Jesus did not continue to grieve. He took action.

Listen: "But didn't I tell you that you will see a wonderful miracle from God if you believe?" Jesus asked her. So they rolled the stone aside. Then Jesus looked up to heaven and said, "Father, thank you for hearing

Me. (You always hear Me, of course, but I said it because of all these people standing here, so that they will believe You sent Me.)" Then He shouted, "Lazarus, come out!" And Lazarus came-bound up in the gravecloth, his face muffled in a head swath. Jesus told them, "Unwrap him and let him go!" JOHN 11:40-44 TLB

It is proper to be sad when we lose a loved one. Jesus was sad but He knew something we should all understand. Not only would he give Lazarus physical life, again, but Jesus knew that Lazarus, because of his faith, would be given eternal life in a perfect place where there are no tears and no suffering.

Listen to a key teaching about death: "The good men perish; the godly die before their time, and no one seems to care or wonder why. No one seems to realize that God is taking them away from evil days ahead. For the godly who die shall rest in peace." ISAIAH 57:1-2 TLB

When we die, we are taken away from evil and delivered to perfection and when those we love die, that is true of them, if they love the Lord. We are simultaneously sad and hopeful. I would have said joyful but that is a word that will fit well when you are reunited with those you love. That is why we tell our family and friends about the love Jesus has for them. We want to be together, in eternity, forever.

"How beautiful upon the mountains are the feet of those who bring the happy news of peace and salvation, the news that the God of Israel reigns. The watchmen shout and sing with joy, for right before their eyes they see the Lord God bring His people home again." ISAIAH 52:7-8 TLB

Discuss ISAIAH 57:1-2. Is it still okay to grieve when someone we love has been taken away from the evil days ahead? For a Christian, is death the end or the beginning? What is transitional and what is permanent? Discuss the meaning of this quotation: "Eye has not seen, nor ear heard, Nor have entered into the heart of man the things which God has prepared for those who love Him." 1 CORINTHIANS 2:9 NKJV

NOTES/REFLECTIONS

CORE VALUE 05

GRACE, FAITH AND WORKS… IN THAT ORDER

> **CORE CHRISTIAN VALUE**
>
> **First God's grace to you, second your faith in Jesus Christ and third, your works, those things you do to respond to His love. We need to know that the order cannot be reversed.**

What is Grace? Grace is a word that describes God's love toward you. The Bible says in 2 PETER 3:8-9TLB "But don't forget this, dear friends that a day or a thousand years from now is like tomorrow to the Lord." He isn't really being slow about His promised return, even though it sometimes seems that way. But He is waiting, for the good reason that He is not willing that any should perish, and He is giving more time for sinners to repent.

That means that God is very serious about His promises and very patient with His children. God does not want one single person to perish, that is, for their spirit to be separated from God and His people, forever. God wants us to repent, that is, to turn away from sin and to love Him, to turn towards Him. But sin did come into the world when Adam was disobedient (with Eve's encouragement). Adam's sin did not surprise God. Nothing ever surprises God. Our God is omniscient, that is, He knows the beginning from the end and He knows what choices man will make.

Since God will not let sin come into His presence, He provided a way for each of us, as well as any person who ever sinned, to be cleansed, to be washed as white as snow so that we could stand in His presence, just as if we had never sinned.

He sent His Son, Jesus, to live a sinless life among men. Jesus, as a result of being hung on a cross by an angry crowd who did not believe He was the Son of God, died. He died that we might, by believing He is the Son of God, be forgiven and cleansed of our sins. All we have to do, to have eternal life, is to humbly and with sorrow confess our sins, to turn away from sin in the future and to rely upon the power of the risen Christ in us so that we can, by faith, experience on a daily basis, God's protective love. Then God expects us to love Him and obey Him.

Some people call the obedience part "works". That just means doing things that God has commanded, such as loving other people, being Baptized, praying to Him about every decision and about our needs and hopes and the needs of others. Works that are rooted in faith please God. Works, simply intended to earn points with God, do not please Him. Faith in Jesus makes your works noticed by God. There you have it! First God's grace to you, second your faith in Jesus Christ and third, your works, those things you do to respond to His love. We need to know that the order cannot be reversed.

Discuss why works alone will not bring you eternal life. For instance, if someone is doing a lot of good things, even going to church and tithing and being good to their neighbor, have they yet done the one thing that makes their works lead to eternal life? Why do you think God's grace must precede faith in Jesus? A way to think about that question is to ask yourselves, "what if God had not sent His only Son to take our sin upon Himself." Could we be in God's presence if our sin was still with us? First, it was God's grace. That means, God's riches at Christ's expense, are ours. Are your good works earning you favor with Jesus or do you do good works because you love Jesus and have faith that He is the Son of God? Do you think good works that are not particularly motivated by your faith in Christ are as meaningful as good works based on your love for Jesus? What do you think it means when the Bible says, "do all things as unto the Lord?"

NOTES/REFLECTIONS

CORE VALUE 06

I AM SO PROUD OF YOU!

> **CORE CHRISTIAN VALUE**
>
> **Pride in oneself misses the point. God gives us gifts (skill, good looks, brains) but those gifts become a test. Give the glory to God when men praise you.**

Have you ever said, to someone you love, "I am so proud of you"! Of course you have and when you said those words, you generally meant that your heart was full of joy for that person. Your pride in who they are and what they have accomplished is a natural and loving response. Can you think of a time in which you would be "proud" of an enemy, someone you did not like and who probably doesn't like you? The answer is generally "no". That is because when you say, "I am so proud of you," you always mean something wholesome and good. You could have said, "My heart is full of joy for you" and meant the same thing. Yet, listen to: PSALM 14:10 "The wicked in his proud countenance does not seek God." NKJV

Here we learn that a person of "proud countenance" has a problem. They are proud of themselves! How can we avoid "pride in ourselves" while accepting the praise and adoration of others? There is a wonderful verse that teaches you how to respond to praise.

"I have been crucified with Christ; it is no longer I who live, but Christ lives in me; and the life which I now live in the flesh I live by faith in the Son of God, who loved me and gave Himself for me." GALATIANS 2:20 NKJV

The only kind of pride we can properly have isn't pride in ourselves but pride in Jesus and the gifts that He has given to us. This kind of pride is centered on "Christ in you" and when people say to you, "I am so proud of you", a mature Christian response is based on the words "I live, yet not I, but Christ lives in me." You can also say "God is so good to me" or "I feel so blessed by God."

You might say to another person, "God has really blessed you with great talent". What we should not say is, "You are so fabulous, better than anyone I know," or anything else that makes the other person feel like, they are the greatest, the fastest, the most talented due to their personal efforts.

Discuss times when people told you how proud they are of you and how you reacted. Should or does your response depend upon who is complimenting you?

Discuss how you can, as a Christian, compliment or praise others.

Discuss what it means when it says "The wicked in his proud countenance does not seek God."

How do the adults in your life handle receiving and giving praise? How about great athletes or performers? Don't let Satan tempt you to take the credit for the gifts of God in your life.

NOTES/REFLECTIONS

CORE VALUE 07

THE TRUST AND FAITH OF A CHILD

> **CORE CHRISTIAN VALUE**
>
> **Jesus repeatedly held up children -their level of trust, their innocence, their faith- as examples of what he wants us all to be.**

If you have ever held a newborn baby you have looked in amazement at what God can do. Even their breath is pure and clean. For the next several years they are dependent on their parents. They must trust their parents to love and protect them. Their innocence will fade as they work their way through life but at least in the beginning they are pure and they are an example of what Jesus wants us to be in our relationship to the Father. Listen to how Jesus discusses the faith of a child as an example of what he expects of adults.

"One day some mothers brought their babies to him to touch and bless. But the disciples told them to go away. Then Jesus called the children over to him and said to the disciples, 'Let the little children come to me! Never send them away! For the Kingdom of God belongs to men who have hearts as trusting as these little children's. And anyone who doesn't have their kind of faith will never get within the Kingdom's gates.'" LUKE 18:15-17 TLB

The next quotation from Jesus makes a point that every parent should not miss. "Take heed that you do not despise one of these little ones, for I say to you that in heaven their angels always see the face of My Father who is in heaven." MATTHEW 18:10 NKJV

Does that verse mean that the child will not suffer from persecution or neglect? No, it means that no matter what the situation, these little ones have an angel watching over them. Jesus also makes it very clear that anyone who harms a child physically or emotionally is in big trouble. Listen:

"But whoever causes one of these little ones who believe in Me to stumble, it would be better for him if a millstone were hung around his neck, and he were thrown into the sea. MARK 9:42-43 NKJV

Have you ever felt like you have or ever had a guardian angel? Why do you think that Jesus used the "faith of a child" as an example of what he expects of us all? Do you now trust God, as you once (and hopefully still do) trusted your parents?

NOTES/REFLECTIONS

CORE VALUE 08

WHAT IS THE BIG DEAL ABOUT READING THE BIBLE?

> **CORE CHRISTIAN VALUE**
>
> God's word is Holy, it is the truth and I need to absorb as much as I can while I can. The entrance of Your word gives light. It will not always be available.

How many people do you think read the Bible very often, often, not often, or hardly at all? If you are among those who read "not often" or "hardly at all", why is that true? Are you able to you know the heart of God without listening to Him? Read what the Bible says about the Word of God.

"For the word of God is living and powerful, and sharper than any two-edged sword, piercing even to the division of soul and spirit, and of joints and marrow, and is a discerner of the thoughts and intents of the heart." HEBREWS 4:11 NKJV

Discuss what the words in that verse mean and then discuss why it would seem unwise to not read the Bible enthusiastically and often. There are many verses that speak to why you should know God's word.

"How can a young man cleanse his way? By taking heed according to Your word. With my whole heart I have sought You; Oh, let me not wander from Your commandments! Your word I have hidden in my heart, that I might not sin against You." PSALM 119:9-11

"I will meditate on Your precepts, And contemplate Your ways. I will delight myself in Your statutes; I will not forget Your word." PSALM 119:15-16 NKJV

The 119th Psalm is full of this kind of admonition and encouragement. Discuss each of the verses you just read. Then, ask yourselves, how important is God's word in your daily life? The Apostle Paul had a student named Timothy. This is what he told the young man:

"Be diligent to present yourself approved to God, a worker who does not need to be ashamed, rightly dividing the word of truth. 2 TIMOTHY 2:15 NKJV

"All Scripture is given by inspiration of God, and is profitable for doctrine, for reproof, for correction, for instruction in righteousness, that the man of God may be complete, thoroughly equipped for every good work." 2 TIMOTHY 3:16-17 NKJV

Listen to the words of the Psalmist: "Your word is a lamp to my feet And a light to my path. The entrance of Your words gives light; I rise before the dawning of the morning, And cry for help; I hope in Your word. My eyes are awake through the night watches, that I may meditate on Your word." PSALM 119:105, 130, 147-148 NKJV Why read early in the morning… you can make it available!

Again, how important is the Word of God to you? Do you sense that a Bible, on a shelf, unstudied, may as well not exist? Discuss ideas about getting more time with the Scriptures. And realize, this: "Behold, the days are coming," says the Lord GOD, "That I will send a famine on the land, not a famine of bread, nor a thirst for water, but of hearing the words of the LORD." AMOS 8:11 NKJV. Discuss what that verse means.

NOTES/REFLECTIONS

CORE VALUE 09

WHO IS IN CHARGE AROUND HERE: GOD OR SATAN?

> **CORE CHRISTIAN VALUE**
>
> God is sovereign and in complete control. God allows Satan to tempt you and to accuse you but God always provides the love, power and support that you need.

To answer that question, let's begin by listening to a conversation between God and Satan.

Now there was a day when the sons of God came to present themselves before the LORD, and Satan also came among them. And the LORD said to Satan, "From where do you come?" So Satan answered the LORD and said, "From going to and fro on the earth, and from walking back and forth on it." Then the LORD said to Satan, "Have you considered My servant Job, that there is none like him on the earth, a blameless and upright man, one who fears God and shuns evil?" So Satan answered the LORD and said, "Does Job fear God for nothing? Have You not made a hedge around him, around his household, and around all that he has on every side? You have blessed the work of his hands, and his possessions have increased in the land. But now, stretch out Your hand and touch all that he has, and he will surely curse You to Your face!" And the LORD said to Satan, "Behold, all that he has is in your power; only do not lay a hand on his person." So Satan went out from the presence of the LORD. JOB 1:6-12 NKJV

We can see, by this excerpt from the book of Job that God is in charge. Whatever power and freedom Satan has comes from God. If you know the entire story of Job, you know a lot about the limitations of Satan's power and the nature of our Lord. God is truly omnipotent (all powerful) omniscient (knows all things) and omnipresent (always present). Yet we know that God allows man to be tempted by Satan. Satan is the tempter, the accuser of man and God allows the test. Discuss the difference between someone who tempts you to sin and One who permits the test. Then listen to the words of Jesus:

"And do not lead us into temptation, but deliver us from the evil one." MATTHEW 6:13 NKJV

Only one entity is in total control. That Entity is our God. Listen:

"Therefore know this day, and consider it in your heart, that the LORD Himself is God in heaven above and on the earth beneath; there is no other." DEUTERONOMY 4:39 NKJV

"Now is the judgment of this world; now the ruler of this world will be cast out. "JOHN 12:31 NKJV

Does it seem like life is a test? Do you know who is tempting you to fail to honor and obey God? To whom must you turn if you are going to successfully endure the tests of life? Listen:

"Be sober, be vigilant; because your adversary the devil walks about like a roaring lion, seeking whom he may devour." 1 PETER 5:8 NKJV. Satan is the accuser but Jesus Christ "in us" is our strength.

Listen to a verse that you should memorize:

There hath no temptation taken you but such as is common to man: but God is faithful, who will not suffer you to be tempted above that ye are able; but will with the temptation also make a way to escape, that ye may be able to bear it. 1 CORINTHIANS 10:13 KJV

NOTES/REFLECTIONS

CORE VALUE 10

WATER BAPTISM IS GOOD; BAPTISM BY THE HOLY SPIRIT IS ESSENTIAL

> **CORE CHRISTIAN VALUE**
>
> Baptism by immersion is both a symbol of our new birth and a public confirmation of our faith. Baptism by the Holy Spirit is a gift of God to all believers.

John the Baptist called people to repent and be baptized. Jesus, who was without sin, did not need to repent but nevertheless He did ask John to baptize Him. John tried to prevent Him, saying, "I need to be baptized by You, and are You coming to me?" …Jesus answered and said to him, "Permit it to be so now, for thus it is fitting for us to fulfill all righteousness." Then he allowed Him." MATTHEW 3:14-15 NKJV

Here Jesus asks John, to baptize Him not because He needed to affirm His repentance, but because it was "to fulfill all righteousness". Jesus was saying that baptism is a confirmation of righteousness and that, in the case of sinners, it represents evidence of their cleansing, their repentance. It also represents a confirmation of the righteousness that comes after repentance.

There are three primary reasons to be baptized. One is that it is evidence of our repentance. Second, it is a public proclamation of our faith in Jesus and finally, it is to do as Jesus did, to follow His example. Then the pursuit of righteousness becomes our life's goal.

Listen to a clear lesson about the baptism of the Holy Spirit: "If a man love Me, he will keep My words: and My Father will love him, and We will come unto him, and make Our abode with him." JOHN 14:23 KJV When we proclaim our love for Jesus and "keep His words" (obey), then the Father and Son will come to live with us.

Listen to what Jesus taught us: "The Helper, the Holy Spirit, whom the Father will send in My name, He will teach you all things, and bring to your remembrance all things that I said to you... when He, the Spirit of truth, has come, He will guide you into all truth."

JOHN 14:26 NKJV

Jesus said to his disciples, "you shall receive power when the Holy Spirit has come upon you; and you shall be witnesses to Me in Jerusalem, and in all Judea and Samaria, and to the end of the earth." ACTS 1:8 NKJV Notice that you shall be witnesses, after the Holy Spirit comes upon you.

Can a person still have the gift of the Holy Spirit if they were never baptized by immersion? (See the story of the thief on cross LUKE 29:43, et. al.). Discuss other possibilities. Do you feel that the Holy Spirit in you is your Comforter, Counselor and Teacher? Is the Holy Spirit a gift or can you earn it? What is the evidence that you have received the Holy Spirit? GALATIANS 5:22-23 NKJV. What do you think Jesus meant when He told Nicodemus that you must be born again? JOHN 3:7 NKJV. Experience God's forgiveness, mercy and love and then be baptized.

NOTES/REFLECTIONS

CORE VALUE 11

SHOULD GENUINE "CARING" FOR SOMEONE PRECEDE WITNESSING TO THEM?

> **CORE CHRISTIAN VALUE**
>
> **Our witness is most effective if the person we are witnessing to knows that we love them and if they can see "Christ in us", a person reborn seeking to be like Jesus.**

Perhaps the best way to approach this question is by posing the opposite view. If you do not like someone and they know that you have no concern for their personal needs, do you feel you can still be an effective witness to them? Probably not. It seems we must first, where the opportunity exists, connect with the person on the human level before they are interested in our spiritual message.

Compassionate, caring behavior opens doors where inconsiderate and unloving behavior slams them shut. But one could ask "what good does it do to be a friend if the friend we are trying to introduce to Jesus, never wants to move our relationship beyond being pals." The Bible provides a response.

"Pursue love, and desire spiritual gifts, but especially that you may prophesy... though I have the gift of prophecy, and understand all mysteries and all knowledge, and though I have all faith, so that I could remove mountains, but have not love, I am nothing." 1 CORINTHIANS 13:2, 14:1 NKJV

To prophesy, as used here, means to teach, to share Christ's love with others. If the person you are trying to witness to does not sense that you love Jesus and them, then your love is incomplete and your witness will be weak. They will know us by our love; no love, no witness. Listen to Paul:

When I was a child, I spoke as a child, I understood as a child, I thought as a child; but when I became a man, I put away childish things. For now we see in a mirror, dimly, but then face to face. Now I know in part, but then I shall know just as I also am known. And now abide faith, hope, love, these three; but the greatest of these is love. 1 CORINTHIANS 13:11-13 NKJV

The Father wants you, His child, to love Him and to tell others of His love for them. When Jesus was asked, what the two most important commandments are, He answered: "'You shall love the LORD your God with all your heart, with all your soul, and with all your mind. This is the first and great commandment. And the second is like it: You shall love your neighbor as yourself. On these two commandments hang all the Law and the Prophets." MATTHEW 22:37-40 NKJV

There you have it. The two greatest commandments are to love God and your neighbor. Love is the light you bring to a relationship. Your love for God shines through and God Himself has enabled you, by the power of the Holy Spirit, to love people that you could never have loved before you knew God. Since Jesus presents you to the Father wrapped in His righteousness, completely cleansed and forgiven, you will find it very logical to extend friendship and support to His children as well. Then they will "hear" you, whether they respond or not. It is our pleasure to witness, not to convert. Conversion is the work of the Holy Spirit in the heart of a new believer.

Discuss persons that you have wanted to witness to but felt that they were not "ready". Then reflect on whether they know you really care for them. Does caring for them mean they have to become perfect in Christ before you will relate to them? Were we perfect in Christ before He came to us? Does it always have to be, "love first, then witness?" Sometimes your love is revealed in your countenance. If you are at peace with the Lord, people will notice. If you have Godly habits, people will notice.

NOTES/REFLECTIONS

CORE VALUE 12

BUT YOU PROMISED... !

> **CORE CHRISTIAN VALUE**
>
> **Promises to God are very serious promises and are called "vows". Make no vows you do not intend to keep because promises to God must be kept; same for vows to your friends and family.**

How many times have you said to someone "but you promised." You were saying that promises count and that a promise should not have been made if you did not mean it. Listen to what the Scriptures have to say about promises (vows, oaths, covenants).

"For when God made a promise to Abraham, because He could swear by no one greater, He swore by Himself, saying, 'Surely blessing I will bless you, and multiplying I will multiply you.' And so, after he had patiently endured, he obtained the promise. For men indeed swear by the greater, and an oath for confirmation is for them an end of all dispute. Thus God, determining to show more abundantly to the heirs of promise the immutability of His counsel, confirmed it by an oath, that by two immutable things, in which it is impossible for God to lie, we might have strong consolation, who have fled for refuge to lay hold of the hope set before us." HEBREWS 6:13-18 NKJV

Here we see that God promised to bless Abraham and his descendants. God also said that since men make oaths which "end all dispute" that His oaths too are immutable, confirmed and that He can not lie. An oath is serious business, not to be entered into lightly. Listen to a key teaching from our Lord about oaths:

"When you make a vow to the LORD your God, you shall not delay to pay it; for the LORD your God will surely require it of you, and it would be sin to you. But if you abstain from vowing, it shall not be sin to you. That which has gone from your lips you shall keep and perform, for you voluntarily vowed to the LORD your God what you have promised with your mouth." DEUTERONOMY 23:21 NKJV. You can see that "oaths not made" are not a problem. In fact, if you abstain from vowing, it is not a sin.

You have heard it said, "I swear, by all that is Holy, I swear on my mother's name and so on." This sort of swearing is also advised against.

"...you have heard that it was said to those of old,' You shall not swear falsely, but shall perform your oaths to the Lord.' But I say to you, do not swear at all: neither by heaven, for it is God's throne; nor by the earth, for it is His footstool; nor by Jerusalem, for it is the city of the great King. Nor shall you swear by your head, because you cannot make one hair white or black. But let your 'Yes' be 'Yes,' and your 'No,' 'No.' For whatever is more than these is from the evil one." MATTHEW 5:33-37 NKJV

God made a promise to Israel as well. "Dwell in this land, and I will be with you and bless you; for to you and your descendants I give all these lands, and I will perform the oath which I swore to Abraham your father. And I will make your descendants multiply as the stars of heaven; I will give to your descendants all these lands; and in your seed all the nations of the earth shall be blessed;" GENESIS 26:3-4 NKJV

Do you tend to make promises that are not necessary? Do you find yourself saying "I swear that is true?" What is the risk in making an oath? Can you think of a way to make a promise in a more tentative way? Is a "conditional: promise okay? Have you heard people say "Lord willing" I will do such and so?

NOTES/REFLECTIONS

CORE VALUE 13

THE DEVIL MADE ME DO IT!

> **CORE CHRISTIAN VALUE**
>
> **As long as we inhabit this mortal body, we will face temptation. But, we never face it alone. God permits the test and as long as we rely on the power of the Holy Spirit, Satan loses.**

A comedian made that line famous but he was only kidding. Here is the truth: ". . . above all, taking the shield of faith with which you will be able to quench all the fiery darts of the wicked one." EPHESIANS 6:16 NKJV. The devil "invites" you to do it, to sin when you know better; but the shield of faith in Jesus allows you to extinguish the fiery darts. The darts are coming, but Jesus, by the power of the Holy Spirit in you, will help you come out victorious.

Commit this verse to memory. You will rely on it often! "There hath no temptation taken you but such as is common to man: but God is faithful, who will not suffer you to be tempted above that ye are able; but will with the temptation also make a way to escape, that ye may be able to bear it." 1 CORINTHIANS 10:13 KJV

"...The Lord knows how to deliver the godly out of temptations" 2 PETER 2:9 NKJV

It is important to know the difference between temptation, always from Satan, and a test, permitted by God. Listen to James, the half brother (same mother) of Jesus: "Let no one say when he is tempted, "I am tempted by God"; for God cannot be tempted by evil, nor does He

Himself tempt anyone. But each one is tempted when he is drawn away by his own desires and enticed." JAMES 1:13 NKJV

Solomon offers some good advice: "O' My son, if sinners entice you, do not consent." PROVERBS 1:10 NKJV

Temptation envelops you if you simply live a common existence. You do not have to look for it, it will look for you. Again James offers a perspective: "My brethren, count it all joy when you fall into various trials, knowing that the testing of your faith produces patience. But let patience have its perfect work, that you may be perfect and complete, lacking nothing." JAMES 1:2 NKJV

You know Jesus was tempted (MATTHEW 4:1-10). That helps you understand that He understands your circumstance, a sort of "been there, experienced that temptation:" situation. I would have said "been there, done that", but Jesus never sinned. Listen: "For in that He Himself has suffered, being tempted, He is able to aid those who are tempted." HEBREWS 2:18 NKJV. Jesus is your strength!

Do you believe that Satan is after your soul? He is indeed. "And the Lord said, Simon, Simon! Indeed, Satan has asked for you, that he may sift you as wheat. But I have prayed for you, that your faith should not fail;" LUKE 22:31 NKJV.

Will you ever, in this life, escape from temptation? Consider how temptations encountered can result in new found strength. Are "you" resisting Satan or is it Christ in you that is enabling you to not sin? Is resisting temptation a scenario where you can say "I live, yet not I, but Christ liveth in me" (GALATIANS 2:20)? Could victory over temptation lead to pride? Whose victory is it? Can temptations lead to greater faith and personal growth?

NOTES/REFLECTIONS

CORE VALUE 14

WITNESSING IS RISKY AND NECESSARY!

> **CORE CHRISTIAN VALUE**
>
> **Jesus charged us with the responsibility to preach the Gospel. That will bring persecution at times. He will not return until the task is accomplished. Just do it.**

The Great Commission: "Go into all the world and preach the gospel to every creature." MARK 16:15 NKJV There is no mistaking the charge. We are to preach the gospel to all the world and to every created person. There is a verse that helps us understand how pivotal this verse is. Listen: "And this gospel of the kingdom will be preached in all the world as a witness to all the nations, and then the end will come." MATTHEW 24:14 NKJV

Do you see that Jesus will not return until the gospel is preached to all nations? It has only been in recent times that the technology exists to make this very possible. For more on this subject visit "A Global Vision" on this site and discuss the possibilities for reaching the whole world, rather quickly.

Who, among the persons you know, is not ready for Jesus to return? Let's read how serious this problem is: "For the time has come for judgment to begin at the house of God; and if it begins with us first, what will be the end of those who do not obey the gospel of God?" 1 PETER 4:17 NKJV.

None of us know, with certainty, the details of what it will be like when disobedient believers and unbelievers are judged by Jesus. We know for sure that it will not be a happy moment. Since Jesus has not yet returned, we still have time to witness of His love to others. But, time is running out.

We feel the sense of urgency that Paul felt: "For if I preach the gospel, I have nothing to boast of, for necessity is laid upon me; yes, woe is me if I do not preach the gospel!" 1 CORINTHIANS 9:16 NKJV Paul goes on to say: "...I am not ashamed of the gospel of Christ, for it is the power of God to salvation for everyone who believes..." ROMANS 1:16 NKJV

Let's clarify a key point. Hearing the Gospel does not necessarily convert anyone. The writer of Hebrews explains: "For indeed the gospel was preached to us as well as to them; but the word which they heard did not profit them, not being mixed with faith in those who heard it." HEBREWS 4:2 NKJV One must have faith in the fact that Jesus was sent by God to redeem all of us and to present us to the Holy Father wrapped in the righteousness of Christ. By God's grace, Jesus was sent, by faith we believe and as a result of God's grace, we seek to serve Him. Hearing those words is not enough. Action is required.

Do you feel that preaching (sharing) the gospel will put you at risk with some of your friends? Listen to what Jesus said: "whoever is ashamed of Me and My words in this adulterous and sinful generation, of him the Son of Man also will be ashamed when He comes in the glory of His Father with the holy angels." MARK 8:38, NKJV

Is "witnessing" always a matter of speaking? Can you think of ways to witness without speaking? If you are weak in your faith how do think the witnessing effort will go? Suppose you have some bad habits that you wish you did not have. Yes, God wants you to be perfect in Him, but does your need for growth permit you to identify with those who also need to grow? Since, as a believer, Jesus has forgiven you and cleansed you, how easy will it be to forgive others for their trespasses, irritable habits, etc. that bother you?

NOTES/REFLECTIONS

CORE VALUE 15

FIDELITY, WHAT IS THAT? A BANK?

> **CORE CHRISTIAN VALUE**
>
> **Fidelity, in the Bible, means being faithful, continuing to trust and love, even in the face of doubts, disappointments and uncertainty. It applies to marriage, both physical and spiritual.**

Given the alarming rate of divorce among Christian and non-Christians, the word "fidelity" has lost some its meaning. Webster says that fidelity is: the quality or state of being faithful. We can not change the past and if your family has experienced a divorce, it is often regrettable and sad but a Christian need not repeat mistakes from lessons learned. Families must move on seeking to be faithful to God and to each other.

From this moment on, focus on fidelity, both to family members, and to our Lord. The scriptures place marriage of persons in the same position as marriage of our spirits with the Spirit of God. Listen: "Let us be glad and rejoice and give Him glory, for the marriage of the Lamb has come, and His wife has made herself ready." REVELATION 19:7 NKJV

The wife described here is the Church, that body of believers who have been made "one" and we are to have true fidelity to the Lamb of God, Jesus and the One who sent Him. Listen to the words from the Book of Hosea:

"I will betroth you to Me forever; Yes, I will betroth you to Me In righteousness and justice, In loving kindness and mercy; I will betroth you to Me in faithfulness, And you shall know the LORD." HOSEA 2:19-20 NKJV

That is God's promise to those who have been "wed" to the Lord. It is a promise He will keep. His fidelity is guaranteed. The Apostle Paul adds more meaning to the definition of marriage:

"Husbands, love your wives, just as Christ also loved the church and gave Himself for her, that He might sanctify and cleanse her with the washing of water by the word, that He might present her to Himself a glorious church, not having spot or wrinkle or any such thing, but that she should be holy and without blemish. So husbands ought to love their own wives as their own bodies; he who loves his wife loves himself. For no one ever hated his own flesh, but nourishes and cherishes it, just as the Lord does the church. For we are members of His body, of His flesh and of His bones. For this reason a man shall leave his father and mother and be joined to his wife, and the two shall become one flesh. This is a great mystery, but I speak concerning Christ and the church. Nevertheless let each one of you in particular so love his own wife as himself, and let the wife see that she respects her husband." EPHESIANS 5:25-33 NKJV

John says, "Then I, John, saw the holy city, New Jerusalem, coming down out of heaven from God, prepared as a bride adorned for her husband" REVELATION 21:2. NKJV This is a ceremony you do not want to miss!

At the human level, is divorce forgivable? It was in the Bible and it is now. Not desirable, but forgivable. So, how important is fidelity in a marriage? Being faithful is critical in our relationship with each other and with our Lord. Discuss why fidelity is such an important concept. Do you think fidelity applies to friendships and relatives? Think of some synonyms that mean the same thing as fidelity.

NOTES/REFLECTIONS

CORE VALUE 16

ISN'T HAVING MONEY A GOOD THING?

> **CORE CHRISTIAN VALUE**
>
> **Blessings are from God and we should use them to bring glory to His name and to show our love to His children. His blessings to us create opportunities for us to be a blessing to others.**

Here is the problem. The Bible says that "...the love of money is the root of all evil." Let's begin with a different approach. Is having money a bad thing? I doubt that anyone would say that having money is a bad thing. For instance, if you had a lot of money could you choose to use it to help others? Of course you could, but you could also choose to keep it all for yourself.

Money is a resource, just as your talent and strength are resources. Some have more than others. If you have more money, talent and strength than someone else, what choices are you making in using your "assets"? Do you wonder if the choice is really yours? Well, it is your choice and the decisions you make show man and God what kind of a person you are. Assets become responsibilities. If you have no assets you have fewer decisions to make in using them. The Bible teaches us that to whom much is given, much is required (LUKE 12:48).

If it turns out that you feel the blessings (money, talent and various kinds of capabilities) are yours, not because God has provided them, but because of your hard work or the work of your parents, then you will be inclined to keep the blessings for yourself. You will use the blessings to build yourself up. You will grow to love the blessings and be fearful of losing them, forgetting that they were a gift from God which could be removed in an instant (earthquake, flood, fire and so on). If you find yourself loving the blessing and fearful of losing it or sharing it with others, you will have missed God's intended purpose for your life.

The Bible teaches that if you love money more than God, you are in trouble (LUKE 16:13). Either serve God with your resources or disappoint God by acting like the resources are for your private enjoyment. If God has given you wonderful blessings it is, in part, because he is watching to see how you use them. Do you notice the needs of others and try to help them or do you love having the blessing so much that you keep it all to yourself? If you have a great deal more than you need, have you thought about why that is true and what God's hopes are for you?

If God has given you blessings, doesn't it make sense to try to be a blessing to others? Having money is a good thing as long as you understand that it is a gift from God. Yes you work hard and you save a portion of your money, but even the energy and talent to work hard is also a gift from God. If God has blessed you, be a pipeline of love to others. Use the assets God has given you to serve Him and to serve others. Little blessings are a little test and huge blessings are a huge test.

Discuss what blessings God has given to each member of the family. Then discuss how you are using those blessings (talent, wealth, wisdom, strength and so on) to be a blessing to others and to bring glory to God. The challenge is this: Does your life bring glory to God? Is God pleased with your efforts to use your blessings to serve Him?

NOTES/REFLECTIONS

CORE VALUE 17

WHO IS YOUR HERO? IS THERE SOMEONE YOU REALLY WANT TO BE LIKE?

> **CORE CHRISTIAN VALUE**
>
> **Jesus, sinless from birth, God's innocent child, lived without sin. It is His perfection we seek; it is Jesus we seek to emulate. He called us friends. Be His friend.**

Do you remember who your first hero was? Probably the trash man (Just love that big noisy truck), a fireman, policeman et. al. When did you switch over to a famous athlete, "Idol" star, or NASCAR driver? Do you know if your heroes love God with all their heart, mind and soul? It would be great if you knew the answer to that question. Those successful people that give God the credit for the wonderful talent and skill they possess are usually worth looking up to.

There are some really important people in the Bible that are "eternal" heroes, that is, they were counted by God, as faithful. Their place in heaven is assured. Therefore, let's look at some things they had to say about their relationship with the Lord. First, James and Jude, two half-brothers of Jesus said almost identical sentences in the opening verse of the books they wrote. "James, a bondservant of God and of the Lord Jesus Christ" and then "Jude, a bondservant of Jesus Christ, and brother of James". They called themselves, bondservants. That meant that they volunteered to dedicate themselves to serving the Lord for the rest of their lives.

When we talk about being servants of our Lord, we may think of that as "not such a great thing, to be a servant." First, service to the Lord is as worship. When you worship, respect and love someone (even your heroes of the past), it is a natural thing to want to be with those that you worship and to attend to their needs and to be a world class fan. Listen to the words of Jesus:

You are My friends if you do whatever I command you. No longer do I call you servants, for a servant does not know what his master is doing; but I have called you friends, for all things that I heard from My Father I have made known to you. JOHN 15:14-15 NKJV

Then Jesus made a commitment to His friends: And He said, "To you it has been given to know the mysteries of the kingdom of God..." LUKE 8:10 NKJV

Daniel was a man who Jesus commends to us several times because of his faith. "I thank You and praise You, O God of my fathers; You have given me wisdom and might,..." DANIEL 2:23 NKJV

These verses make it clear that Jesus reveals mysteries and gives wisdom and strength to His friends. JAMES 2:23 says "...Abraham believed God, and it was accounted to him for righteousness." And he was called the friend of God.

Do you feel Jesus is your personal friend? Discuss the things that would indicate that He is your friend. If you have to have a hero in this life, think of one person that you count worthy. What is there about that friend that is unique? Who is the one true friend that will never leave you or forsake you, One that was sinless and the perfect role model? Remember the WWJD motto? Of course it stood for What Would Jesus Do and that motto works. You can ask Jesus for advice and leadership in your life, constantly.

NOTES/REFLECTIONS

CORE VALUE 18

HOW CAN I FEEL JOYFUL WHEN MY LIFE AND THE WORLD AROUND ME ARE FALLING APART?

> **CORE CHRISTIAN VALUE**
>
> **Joy is the condition of a believer's life. Not joy in suffering or rejection, but joy in knowing that through every circumstance the Holy Spirit is with you, comforting and guiding you.**

First, let's understand what God prescribes in a Psalm from David: "... let all those rejoice who put their trust in You; Let them ever shout for joy, because You defend them; Let those also who love Your name Be joyful in You. For You, O LORD, will bless the righteous; With favor You will surround him as with a shield." PSALM 5:11-12 NKJV

In the midst of difficult circumstances, how can you possibly be "full of joy"? If you are not a Christian, empowered by the Holy Spirit in you, the answer is that, in all probability, you can not. Look carefully at the verse above. Those who put their trust in the Lord, rejoice. Those who are defended by God shout for joy. Those who love the name of God are joyful, in Him. The verse says that the Lord will bless the righteous and surround you with a shield and favor you. Yes, trials will come but you are never going through them alone if you love the Lord. What can you focus on if you feel alone and are hurting?

People who are depressed and sad, even though they love the Lord, are sometimes experiencing pain, mental and/or physical and the pain is real. Jesus experienced pain and rejection. Listen:

"…(Jesus Christ) made Himself of no reputation, taking the form of a bondservant, and coming in the likeness of men. And being found in appearance as a man, He humbled Himself and became obedient to the point of death, even the death of the cross. Therefore God also has highly exalted Him and given Him the name which is above every name, that at the name of Jesus every knee should bow, of those in heaven, and of those on earth, and of those under the earth, and that every tongue should confess that Jesus Christ is Lord, to the glory of God the Father." PHILIPPIANS 2:7-11 NKJV

He who suffered for us, joyfully presents us to the Father, cleansed of our sin. These verses tell it all: "… when they had called for the apostles and beaten them, they commanded that they should not speak in the name of Jesus, and let them go. So they departed from the presence of the council, rejoicing that they were counted worthy to suffer shame for His name. And daily in the temple, and in every house, they did not cease teaching and preaching Jesus as the Christ." ACTS 5:40-42 NKJV

"Who shall bring a charge against God's elect? It is God who justifies. Who is he who condemns? It is Christ who died, and furthermore is also risen, who is even at the right hand of God, who also makes intercession for us. Who shall separate us from the love of Christ? Shall tribulation, or distress, or persecution, or famine, or nakedness, or peril, or sword?…For I am persuaded that neither death nor life, nor angels nor principalities nor powers, nor things present nor things to come, nor height nor depth, nor any other created thing, shall be able to separate us from the love of God which is in Christ Jesus our Lord…….. ROMANS 8:33-39. Draw near to God and He will draw near to you. JAMES 4:8 NKJV

Jesus knows our circumstances. Do you feel His presence in all things at all times? Whether you do or not, His Spirit is always present. Is it okay to feel sad? Listen to James, Jesus' brother: My brethren, count it all joy when you fall into various trials, knowing that the testing of your faith produces patience. Yes we will feel sad and depressed but the power of the Holy Spirit will lift your spirit.

NOTES/REFLECTIONS

CORE VALUE 19

WHO IS GOING TO EXPLAIN THE SCRIPTURES TO ME?

> **CORE CHRISTIAN VALUE**
>
> **The Holy Scriptures are God's gift to us. Let no man contradict or deny the Word. God's Spirit in you is the interpreter. His Light shines in your heart as a star in the darkness. Seek Him.**

In today's world, there are many people willing to tell you what they think God wants you to know. Many of these teachers, priests, pastors and prophets are very sincere and they can be of great assistance to you. But, in the final analyses, we have the most wonderful, perfect Teacher that exists. We have the prophetic Word. Listen:

"All Scripture is given by inspiration of God, and is profitable for doctrine, for reproof, for correction, for instruction in righteousness, that the man of God may be complete, thoroughly equipped for every good work." 2 TIMOTHY 3:16 NKJV

God's word is the final word. It equips you that you may be "complete", thoroughly equipped. What a wonderful promise. You are now able to use God's word to establish your own personal relationship with Him. He becomes your teacher. Memorize this verse. It is a daily reality! "Your word is a lamp to my feet and a light to my path." PSALM 119:105 "Lead me in paths of righteousness" PSALM 23:3 can be your constant prayer.

As to the "interpretation of the word", listen: "And so we have the prophetic word confirmed, which you do well to heed as a light that shines in a dark place, until the day dawns and the morning star rises in your hearts; knowing this first, that no prophecy of Scripture is of any private interpretation, for prophecy never came by the will of man, but holy men of God spoke as they were moved by the Holy Spirit." 2 PETER 1:19-21 NKJV

How trustworthy and useful is His word. Listen: "The law of the LORD is perfect, converting the soul; The testimony of the LORD is sure, making wise the simple; The statutes of the LORD are right, rejoicing the heart; The commandment of the LORD is pure, enlightening the eyes; The fear of the LORD is clean, enduring forever; The judgments of the LORD are true and righteous altogether. More to be desired are they than gold, Yea, than much fine gold; Sweeter also than honey and the honeycomb. Moreover by them Your servant is warned, And in keeping them there is great reward." PSALM 19:7-11 NKJV

When is the right time to learn the word? Again the answer is before us. "From childhood you have known the Holy Scriptures, which are able to make you wise for salvation through faith which is in Christ Jesus."

2 TIMOTHY 3:15 NKJV

What steps can you take to "Store God's word in your heart that you might not sin against Him?" How can we access God's wisdom? If there is a dispute as to the meaning of a verse, to what or to whom do you look for insight? What does it mean when it says, "I am the light of the world. He who follows Me shall not walk in darkness, but have the light of life." JOHN 8:12 NKJV Do you feel you have the Light within you? How does one "turn on the light"?

NOTES/REFLECTIONS

CORE VALUE 20

I AM SOOOOO MAD!

> **CORE CHRISTIAN VALUE**
>
> **Do not let the sun set on a family disagreement. God's will for our lives is harmony with Him and each other. Anger is a tool of Satan. Do not let him win.**

Too often we are angry about something. It is not that anger is an unreasonable response in some situations. Jesus got angry when the "money changers" were misusing the Temple to do business. But, we are not the righteous, sinless Son of God. He teaches us the following:

"But I say to you that whoever is angry with his brother without a cause shall be in danger of the judgment. And whoever says to his brother, 'Raca!' shall be in danger of the council. But whoever says,' You fool!' shall be in danger of hell fire. Therefore if you bring your gift to the altar, and there remember that your brother has something against you, leave your gift there before the altar, and go your way. First be reconciled to your brother, and then come and offer your gift." MATTHEW 5:22-24 NKJV "Let no corrupt word proceed out of your mouth, but what is good for necessary edification, that it may impart grace to the hearers. And do not grieve the Holy Spirit of God, by whom you were sealed for the day of redemption. Let all bitterness, wrath, anger, clamor, and evil speaking be put away from you, with all malice. And be kind to one another, tenderhearted, forgiving one another, even as God in Christ forgave you." EPHESIANS 4: 29-32 NKJV

You have just read the "basics" about anger. Call no man a fool, don't come to God with a gift if you are angry with a brother, speak in a way that edifies, builds up and imparts grace to others and do not grieve the Holy Spirit by being angry. No bitterness, bad temper and evil speaking should overtake you. Be kind, tenderhearted and forgive others just as Jesus has forgiven you. Do you think you can do these things in and of your own strength? I assure you, our "lower nature", our sinful flesh "rules" unless you consciously decide that does not need to be the case. It grieves our Lord when you cave in and get angry! The Holy Spirit in you is the only way you will ever cope with anger.

A man I know told his children the following verse every time they would get ready to go to bed, mad: "Be angry, and do not sin: do not let the sun go down on your wrath, nor give place to the devil." EPHESIANS 4:26-27 NKJV. Then he would make them give each other a hug and say they were sorry. Now maybe they were not truly sorry but they never forgot the lesson. Don't let the sun go down on your anger because when you do you are giving the devil the victory. King David said, "Cease from anger, and forsake wrath; Do not fret – it only causes harm." Anger hurts both sides. Do you feel there is victory in "beating up" on someone physically or mentally?

Listen to Jesus' brother, James: "But the wisdom that is from above is first pure, then peaceable, gentle, willing to yield, full of mercy and good fruits, without partiality and without hypocrisy. Now the fruit of righteousness is sown in peace by those who make peace." JAMES 3:17-18 NKJV.

Paul said "But now you yourselves are to put off all these: anger, wrath, malice, blasphemy, filthy language out of your mouth." COLOSSIANS 3:8 NKJV.

Discuss how you have successfully handled anger or when and why you failed to do so. Is this topic a sort of microcosm, a small scale, of the whole battle between your tendency to sin and your desire to be like Jesus? What steps can be taken to win this battle?

NOTES/REFLECTIONS

CORE VALUE 21

FINALLY, ALL THIS STUFF IS MINE!

> **CORE CHRISTIAN VALUE**
>
> Everything that we see is "temporary", it will cease to exist. The things we do not yet see are "eternal" and will never cease to exist. Don't get too attached to anything in this world!

No, the things we accumulate are not ours. They are on loan so to speak. God provides many wonderful gifts and assets for our use. Not one thing exists or is made that wasn't provided by God. We think we "invent" things but the things we invent are made up of what God has provided. God has been very generous with us. Look around at all the "stuff" we have to use and enjoy. Of course, what we see is much more than what we have made with God's resources. Many feel that nature, undisturbed by man, is the greatest gift, the most amazing resource. When you are alone with God in nature, thinking about Him and His creation, it is a special moment whether on a mountain top or by the sea.

One of the most instructive things Jesus did was show us how He chose to be alone with the Father. Luke said of Jesus: "He Himself often withdrew into the wilderness and prayed." Luke 5:16. NKJV Going away from people to be alone with God is refreshing and intense. You feel like you are drawing close to Him, talking to Him and listening to Him. When the Scriptures refer to God and Jesus as the "I am", the I Am is omnipresent, omniscient and omnipotent. Discuss what those three words mean and why they take on new meaning when you are alone with God in nature. If the resources created for our use by God are temporary, does it not make sense that God has prepared a better place? Listen to the writer of Hebrews and to Paul: "But now they desire a better, that is, a heavenly country. Therefore God is not ashamed to be called their God, for He has prepared a city for them." Hebrews 11:16 "For here we have no continuing city, but we seek the one to come." Hebrews 13:14 NKJV

"For our citizenship is in heaven, from which we also eagerly wait for the Savior, the Lord Jesus Christ, who will transform our lowly body that it may be conformed to His glorious body, according to the working by which He is able even to subdue all things to Himself." Philippians 3:20, 21 NKJV

Yes, there is a better place where all resources, including us, will abide. We get pretty worked up over protecting our resources here on earth and for good reason if that includes protecting and respecting what God has created. But it is clear enough that which we can not yet see will be wonderful. Listen again to Paul: "Eye has not seen, nor ear heard, nor have entered into the heart of man the things which God has prepared for those who love Him." 1 Corinthians 2:9 NKJV

That is a very big statement, followed by these verses: "But God has revealed them to us through His Spirit. For the Spirit searches all things, yes, the deep things of God. For what man knows the things of a man except the spirit of the man which is in him? Even so no one knows the things of God except the Spirit of God. Now we have received, not the spirit of the world, but the Spirit who is from God, that we might know the things that have been freely given to us by God." 1 Corinthians 2:10-12 NKJV

Does the fact that all things on earth will perish bother you? Discuss this difficult question carefully and then move to why these things exist. Will the Garden of Eden, the perfect place, be restored? Where, if you had to guess? How can you know the "deep things of God"?

NOTES/REFLECTIONS

CORE VALUE 22

CAN A FIG TREE YIELD OLIVES?

> **CORE CHRISTIAN VALUE**
>
> Evil people yield "fruit" and Christian's yield "fruit." If we claim to be a Christian, our lives should yield the fruit of the Holy Spirit.

This question is answered by James, the half-brother of Jesus: "Does a spring send forth fresh water and bitter from the same opening? Can a fig tree, my brethren, bear olives, or a grapevine bear figs? Thus no spring yields both salt water and fresh." JAMES 3: 11-12 NKJV

No, a fig tree will never bear olives nor should a Christian bear fruit that is not consistent with the teachings of our Lord. Listen to the words of Jesus:

"For a good tree does not bear bad fruit, nor does a bad tree bear good fruit. For every tree is known by its own fruit. For men do not gather figs from thorns, nor do they gather grapes from a bramble bush. A good man out of the good treasure of his heart brings forth good; and an evil man out of the evil treasure of his heart brings forth evil. For out of the abundance of the heart his mouth speaks." LUKE 6:43-45 NKJV

It is clear that Jesus is teaching us that our lives should bear fruit that glorify Him. We should not say we love Jesus in one breath and curse mankind in the next breath. Jesus says that the good treasure in our heart should bring forth good and that out of the abundance of our heart, we speak. A heart that loves the Lord will seek to serve Jesus and will do things with their life that prove their faith is real.

How does one get a heart that loves the Lord? Listen again to Jesus: "Repentance leads to the acquisition of the Fruits of the Spirit or it was not repentance." MATTHEW 3:10 Here Jesus is teaching us that repentance is the key. Confess your sins, be baptized and turn from sin of every kind and the fruits of the Spirit are yours. Jesus clarifies that point in Matthew when he says, "seek first the kingdom of God and His righteousness, and all these things shall be added to you." MATTHEW 6:33 NKJV

Notice that seeking the kingdom of God, precedes his gifts. First seek, then find, knowing that these things are "added" unto you. We can not earn our salvation, or simply acquire the fruits of Spirit by willing it to be so; it is a gift from God, added to us by His grace. Now listen to what Paul said about our new nature, in Christ, as he names the fruit of the Spirit.

"...the fruit of the Spirit is love, joy, peace, longsuffering, kindness, goodness, faithfulness, gentleness, self-control. Against such there is no law." GALATIANS 5:22-23 NKJV. I strongly recommend that you memorize the fruits of the Spirit. They represent your daily yardstick; they measure your behavior.

How hard is it to be like Jesus? Is there a pivotal strength that enables you? Can you take credit for this strength in you? Will people know you love Jesus as they observe your actions, words and countenance? How important is it to bear fruit that confirms your love of Jesus and your fellow man?

NOTES/REFLECTIONS

CORE VALUE 23

WHEN DID GOD GRIEVE BECAUSE OF ME?

> **CORE CHRISTIAN VALUE**
>
> **When we speak with bitterness or anger and are unkind to one another, it grieves the Holy Spirit of God. Our sins grieve our parents, us and God. There is no upside in sinful behavior!**

Any loving parent, when they observe their child being very ill behaved, is very disappointed. That disappointment may look like anger, but at its deeper roots, it is grief triggered by the child's failure to do the right thing. If you can understand that fact, it is a small step to understand that when we, the children of God, are bitter and angry, it grieves our heavenly Father.

Listen to Paul's admonition to us all: "Let no corrupt word proceed out of your mouth, but what is good for necessary edification, that it may impart grace to the hearers. And do not grieve the Holy Spirit of God, by whom you were sealed for the day of redemption. Let all bitterness, wrath, anger, clamor, and evil speaking be put away from you, with all malice. And be kind to one another, tenderhearted, forgiving one another, even as God in Christ forgave you." EPHESIANS 4:29-32 NKJV

The good news here is that we were "sealed for the day of redemption" even though we grieved the Holy Spirit but the Scriptures go on to say that our actions, after our redemption is sealed, count. Do you realize that your moment by moment thoughts and actions "count"?

Therefore thus says the Lord GOD to them: "Behold, I Myself will judge between the fat and the lean sheep. Because you have pushed with side and shoulder, butted all the weak ones with your horns, and scattered them abroad, therefore I will save My flock, and they shall no longer be a prey; and I will judge between sheep and sheep. EZEKIEL 34:20-23 NKJV

God Himself will judge between the sheep and the sheep, that is, He will judge between believers. The goats will have first been judged by Jesus and His angels (MATTHEW 35:31-33) and they, because they are classified as non-believers, are in big trouble. But the point here is that our actions "count", once we are judged as believers, seeking to be obedient and loving towards God and our fellow man.

It seems that the "grief" God feels is directed towards believers who have disappointed Him. My guess is that we will all, to some degree, disappoint God because we are imperfect. Rather than "beat yourself up" over your mistakes, resolve to make fewer mistakes. There is an old hymn entitled, Trust and Obey. That is the simple truth. God will grieve less and less about you if you are striving to be like Jesus.

If God knows you as His child, do you realize that when you are being "bad" in some sense of the word, that you are grieving not only your parents but your God as well? How much incentive is it for you to "do the right thing", if "doing the wrong thing" grieves God? Do you feel you "sin" in secret? What do you think it means when the Bible says, "I, the LORD, search the heart, I test the mind, even to give every man according to his ways, according to the fruit of his doings. JEREMIAH 17:10 NKJV

NOTES/REFLECTIONS

CORE VALUE 24

DID I CHOOSE GOD OR DID HE CHOOSE ME? YES! AND YES!

> **CORE CHRISTIAN VALUE**
>
> We are "elected" by God to be His children; the Word (in 1 TIMOTHY 2:4 NKJV) says, "God our Savior…desires all men to be saved and to come to the knowledge of the truth." Do it.

When we talk about the issue of choosing to follow God and being filled with His Spirit, it is critical to understand two facts. The first is stated by Jesus. Listen. "You did not choose Me, but I chose you and appointed you that you should go and bear fruit, and that your fruit should remain." JOHN 15:16 then Paul says, 14 "for when Gentiles, who do not have the law (of Moses), by nature do the things in the law, these, although not having the law, are a law to themselves, 15 who show the work of the law written in their hearts, their conscience also bearing witness, and between themselves their thoughts accusing or else excusing them." ROMANS 2:14-16 NKJV

Yes God chose you and yes you responded because He placed the truth in your heart. Did God know you would or would not respond to His call? Yes, but you, in this physical body, limited by time and space, do not know the Alpha from the Omega, the beginning from the end. God does! He sees you now and then, before you were born and in eternity. Nothing you do surprises God. He knew the choices you would make. Do you feel you are free to reject God? Yes you are but God knows, even now, your final circumstance. He chose you! Now, you respond to His love …or not.

God made it easy for you, in a sense. Listen to the teaching of the Apostle John: "…the anointing which you have received from Him abides in you, and you do not need that anyone teach you; but as the same anointing teaches you concerning all things, and is true, and is not a lie, and just as it has taught you, you will abide in Him. 1 JOHN 2:27 NKJV

You read, up above, that your thoughts excuse you or accuse you. That is because God gave you a conscience, the Truth in you. That is why those who reject God will be without excuse. Listen to an explanation by Paul: 19 "because what may be known of God is manifest in them, for God has shown it to them. 20 For since the creation of the world His invisible attributes are clearly seen, being understood by the things that are made, even His eternal power and Godhead, so that they are without excuse", ROMANS 1:19-20 NKJV

First, the Father and Son chose you and secondly, you responded, just as They, the Holy Trinity, knew you would. They, the Father, Son and Holy Spirit placed the truth on your heart and you responded or not. God wants you to respond positively. He wants you to spend eternity with Him.

Does it bother you that God knows your final circumstance and you may not? Certainty is at your doorstep! Do you ever wonder about whether you truly know right from wrong? When there are questions, where do you turn for answers? Allow me to offer a hint; "Thy Word I have hid in my heart that I might not sin against you." Can the Word of God become a point of reference for you if you do not read and study it? The Bible is God's Word, written for you. It is God speaking to you through the words of Jesus, the prophets and the apostles. The interpreter is the Holy Spirit in you.

NOTES/REFLECTIONS

CORE VALUE 25

THE MYSTERY OF THE HOLY SPIRIT, REVEALED

> **CORE CHRISTIAN VALUE**
>
> There are three that bear witness in heaven: The Father, The Word and The Holy Spirit and these three are one. Jesus is the Word, the Light sent from God, the Holy Spirit, sent.

We are now in physical bodies. We have a spirit and Jesus made it possible, by his atoning sacrifice (taking our sins upon Himself), for our spirit to be united with His Spirit. Since we know all physical bodies will die it is important to know that our spiritual selves do not die. Our spirits will live on, either separated from God or joined with God. If we make the choice to join our spirit with His Spirit, then from that time on we have the gift of the Holy Spirit (this is a choice God calls us to and one He knew we would make because He is omniscient, he knows all things including every action and thought of every person from the beginning of time and for eternity).

What is the Trinity? It is sometimes difficult for us to know whether to pray to God, to Jesus or to the Holy Spirit. When you pray do you tend to say "Father" or "Lord" or "Jesus" or "Holy Spirit? Which is right? They are all correct because all are present all of the time awaiting your prayers. John teaches us that the Father, Son and Holy Spirit are "One". "For there are three that bear witness in heaven: the Father, the Word, and the Holy Spirit; and these three are one." I JOHN 5:7 NKJV

The Holy Spirit is an entity, sent by the Father and the Son to abide in us constantly and forever. It is this Holy Spirit in us that gives us the strength, courage and will to be like Jesus. It helps us love God with all our hearts, mind and soul and to love our neighbors as ourselves. The Holy Spirit in you is an "eternal" condition. Jesus said, "Go therefore and make disciples of all the nations, baptizing them in the name of the Father and of the Son and of the Holy Spirit..." MATTHEW 28:19 NKJV

This next verse presents a preview, so to speak, of what God intends for each of us: "When He had been baptized, Jesus came up immediately from the water; and behold, the heavens were opened to Him, and He saw the Spirit of God descending like a dove and alighting upon Him. And suddenly a voice came from heaven, saying "This is My beloved Son, in whom I am well pleased." MATTHEW 3:16-17 NKJV. When you are baptized in water you are following the example of Jesus and the Father will send the Holy Spirit to you as you declare your discipleship.

I speculate, but doves seem to always be around and I know the Holy Spirit is always present in me but the doves seem to be reminding me that He is present. I feel the same way about a gentle breeze. Have you ever felt the presence of the Spirit in the comforting caress of the gentle breeze? Listen to the words of Jesus: "The wind blows where it wishes, and you hear the sound of it, but cannot tell where it comes from and where it goes. So is everyone who is born of the Spirit." JOHN 3:8 NKJV

"For what man knows the things of a man except the spirit of the man which is in him? Even so no one knows the things of God except the Spirit of God. Now we have received, not the spirit of the world, but the Spirit who is from God, that we might know the things that have been freely given to us by God." 1 CORINTHIANS 2:11-12 NKJV. Do you know that God sends the Holy Spirit to teach and guide you? Discuss times that you felt the presence of the Holy Spirit. How can God be omnipresent, constantly in you and around you? Jesus called the Holy Spirit the comforter, helper, teacher, counselor, the Spirit of truth, dwelling in you. You are no longer an orphan! (JOHN Ch. 14 & 15)

NOTES/REFLECTIONS

CORE VALUE 26

WHEN THE BIBLE SPEAKS OF "BLASPHEMY" WHAT DOES THAT MEAN?

> **CORE CHRISTIAN VALUE**
>
> **The blasphemy of the Holy Spirit is the only sin in the Bible characterized as "unforgivable". A true believer should never expect the re-enactment of the crucifixion, for his sins.**

Merriam-Webster defines it as follows: 1 a: the act of insulting or showing contempt or lack of reverence for God. b: the act of claiming the attributes of deity. 2: irreverence toward something considered sacred or inviolable.

Now listen to the words of Jesus: "Therefore I say to you, every sin and blasphemy will be forgiven men, but the blasphemy against the Spirit will not be forgiven men. 32 Anyone who speaks a word against the Son of Man, it will be forgiven him; but whoever speaks against the Holy Spirit, it will not be forgiven him, either in this age or in the age to come." MATTHEW 12:31-32 NKJV

Why would Jesus single out blasphemy of the Holy Spirit as the only unforgivable sin? Listen to the words of the writer of the book of Hebrews: "For it is impossible for those who were once enlightened, and have tasted the heavenly gift, and have become partakers of the Holy Spirit, and have tasted the good word of God and the powers of the age to come, if they fall away, to renew them again to repentance, since they crucify again for themselves the Son of God, and put Him to an open shame." HEBREWS 6:4-6 NKJV

These teachings make it very clear that blasphemy of the Holy Spirit is a fatal offense. In my opinion, once you have known the peace of Jesus and have experienced His cleansing, forgiveness and love, if you then were to then have contempt for our Lord and God, it would indeed be something that borders on mental illness. To have truly known Him and then to insult Him, makes no sense at all. It is far more likely that if you have claimed to have been born again and then "intentionally insult" the Holy Spirit, the power of Christ in you, in a conscious, hateful manner, you never really entered into His peace and He never really was your indwelling Lord.

Salvation is not for sissies. Do not timidly and half-heartedly seek Him. It would be like getting married and then telling your spouse, "I did not really mean it when I said our vows." Jesus is teaching us that He went to the cross to die for our sins and once was enough! Do not, as it says in Hebrews, ask Jesus to go to the cross again and again, putting Him to open shame.

Listen to a description of the soul of one who is saved: "Come now, and let us reason together," Says the LORD, "Though your sins are like scarlet, They shall be as white as snow; Though they are red like crimson, They shall be as wool. ISAIAH 1:18 NKJV

Jesus has cleansed us and will, because of His eternal love for us, continue to cleanse us and empower us via the Holy Spirit. Do you sense His empowerment? Where do you turn for wisdom? Do you understand what it means when it says blasphemy is unforgivable? Discuss the many ways that the world tempts you to deny your Lord.

NOTES/REFLECTIONS

CORE VALUE 27

AND THE GREATEST COMMANDMENT IS .. ?

> **CORE CHRISTIAN VALUE**
>
> There are 10 commandments. The first 4 pertain to God and the remaining 6 pertain to man. Jesus summarized them and said, "Love God with all your heart, mind, strength and soul and your neighbor as yourself."

We sometimes struggle with complex requirements of obedience in the Scriptures but in the case of knowing what the two greatest commandments are in the Bible, Jesus made it very simple. In response to a scribe's (lawyer) question, "Which is the first commandment of all?" Jesus answered him, "The first of all the commandments is: 'Hear, O Israel, the LORD our God, the LORD is one. And you shall love the LORD your God with all your heart, with all your soul, with all your mind, and with all your strength.' This is the first commandment. And the second, like it, is this: 'You shall love your neighbor as yourself.' There is no other commandment greater than these."MARK 12:28-31 NKJV

When we study the 10 commandments, we find that the first 4 that are listed point us to loving God and the second 6 concern our relationships with man.

When you think about the commandments, they represent a very tight summary of what we are expected to do as children of God. We do not obey these commandments "to become" children of God, we obey them because we are God's children. He gives us His grace that we might know Him and then we, by faith, obey Him. Our obedience does not "earn us anything"; it is simply our response to His love for us. We do know that disobedience will bring discipline but there is a big difference between a disobedient person that does not know God and does not love Him and one who does know Him and loves Him. This is a critical point to understand. God calls you to Him. He calls all men and would that none perish. But, some do not respond. Your response to His grace, His call to you, is a response of faith, one of believing in Jesus Christ and what He did that enables us to come into God's presence completely cleansed of our sin.

Then we endeavor to obey, relying upon the power of the Holy Spirit in us, to help us be more and more like Jesus, every day. Our obedience to the two greatest commandments is important. Discuss the 10 commandments. Which do you feel are most difficult to obey? Which is easiest? Do you think there will ever come a time in your Christian growth where you will "automatically" obey, without thinking about it? That process is called sanctification. The Bible refers to believers as saints. How far do you feel from that designation?

THE TEN COMMANDMENTS

Pertaining to God:

1. Thou shalt have no other gods before Me
2. Thou shalt not worship any graven images
3. Thou shalt not take the name of God in vain
4. Remember the Sabbath to keep it holy

Pertaining to Man:

5. Honor thy father and thy mother
6. Thou shalt not kill
7. Thou shalt not commit adultery
8. Thou shalt not steal
9. Thou shalt not bear false witness
10. Thou shalt not covet thy neighbor

NOTES/REFLECTIONS

CORE VALUE 28

ARE YOU A FOXHOLE CHRISTIAN?

> **" CORE CHRISTIAN VALUE**
>
> God does not intend that the Light within us be hidden. "For you were once darkness, but now you are light in the Lord. Walk as children of light." **EPHESIANS 5:8 NKJ**

Miriam-Webster defines a foxhole as: a pit dug usually hastily for individual cover from enemy fire. When you are feeling attacked because of your Christian faith and beliefs, do you sometimes feel like hiding in a foxhole? Some of us often do and that is a natural reaction. We do not like sticking our neck out when we are being attacked for our beliefs. There is another military expression that one sometimes hears; there are Christians who "fly under the radar". They live life in such a way that they are as a phantom Christian. No one knows they are a Christian! Are you anxious for people to know that you love the Lord; or, would you prefer that your faith be a private affair? There are a lot of people whose lives seem to indicate that they do not want to make other people "uncomfortable" by declaring their faith, either by their actions or their words.

The Bible indicates that if you "live for Christ", at some point you will suffer persecution. Listen to Paul's teaching to Timothy. "Yes, and all who desire to live godly in Christ Jesus will suffer persecution." 2 TIMOTHY 3:12 NKJV. Then Jesus makes the same point: "Blessed are those who are persecuted for righteousness' sake, for theirs is the kingdom of heaven." MATTHEW 5:10 NKJV Do you feel persecuted for your faith? Is it possible that you are being persecuted and do not realize it? If you know you are being persecuted because of your faith, listen to words of Paul: "Who shall separate us from the love of Christ? Shall tribulation, or distress, or persecution, or famine, or nakedness, or peril, or sword?" ROMANS 8:35 NKJV. Again, Paul puts our persecution in perspective: "Yet in all these things we are more than conquerors through Him who loved us. For I am persuaded that neither death nor life, nor angels nor principalities nor powers, nor things present nor things to come, nor height nor depth, nor any other created thing, shall be able to separate us from the love of God which is in Christ Jesus our Lord." ROMANS 8:37-39 NKJV

Jesus made our persecution seem certain. Listen: "Remember the word that I said to you, 'A servant is not greater than his master.' If they persecuted Me, they will also persecute you." JOHN 15:20 NKJV. I am sure we will not all experience the same sort of persecution but listen to one group's circumstance: "Then I saw the souls of those who had been beheaded for their witness to Jesus and for the word of God, who had not worshiped the beast or his image, and had not received his mark on their foreheads or on their hands. And they lived and reigned with Christ for a thousand years." REVELATION 20:4 NKJV Listen to excellent advice from Peter. "But even if you should suffer for righteousness' sake, you are blessed. And do not be afraid of their threats, nor be troubled. But sanctify the Lord God in your hearts, and always be ready to give a defense to everyone who asks you a reason for the hope that is in you, with meekness and fear; having a good conscience, that when they defame you as evildoers, those who revile your good conduct in Christ may be ashamed. For it is better, if it is the will of God, to suffer for doing good than for doing evil." 1 PETER 3:14-17 NKJV

What might be an appropriate response to persecution? Discuss times that you knew you were being persecuted, because of your testimony and faith. What if you have never felt persecution? Why not?

NOTES/REFLECTIONS

CORE VALUE 29

A "SIPPY CUP" APPROACH TO GROWTH!

> **CORE CHRISTIAN VALUE**
>
> **When we first seek a relationship with our Lord, we do so as "babes" and we feed upon the milk of the word. We must not remain infants. As we grow in the word, we mature in Christ.**

"Whom will he teach knowledge? And whom will he make to understand the message? Those just weaned from milk? Those just drawn from the breasts? For precept must be upon precept, precept upon precept, Line upon line, line upon line, Here a little, there a little." ISAIAH 28:9-10 NKJV

Here you see that Isaiah is saying that knowledge and understanding are not gained by infants. They must grow, little by little. Listen to how the writer of Hebrews makes the same point:

"For though by this time you ought to be teachers, you need someone to teach you again the first principles of the oracles of God; and you have come to need milk and not solid food. For everyone who partakes only of milk is unskilled in the word of righteousness, for he is a babe. But solid food belongs to those who are of full age, that is, those who by reason of use have their senses exercised to discern both good and evil." HEBREWS 5:12-14 NKJV

It is clear enough that there are two kinds of students of the word described here. There are those who can digest milk only, that is, the meal an infant can handle and there are those who can digest meat as an adult. Which kind of student of the word are you? Do you feel more like an infant or an adult? To the degree that you feel immature in the word, you have a solution at hand. Listen to Paul's teaching:

"When I was a child, I spoke as a child, I understood as a child, I thought as a child; but when I became a man, I put away childish things. For now we see in a mirror, dimly, but then face to face. Now I know in part, but then I shall know just as I also am known." 1 CORINTHIANS 13:11-13 NKJV

Paul points you toward the time when your dim vision of that which you will eventually know, will be made clear when you are in heaven. Even spiritually mature persons only have a dim vision of what is coming. Listen again to Paul describe what is coming: "…till we all come to the unity of the faith and of the knowledge of the Son of God, to a perfect man, to the measure of the stature of the fullness of Christ; that we should no longer be children, tossed to and fro and carried about with every wind of doctrine, by the trickery of men, in the cunning craftiness of deceitful plotting, but, speaking the truth in love, may grow up in all things into Him who is the head – Christ – EPHESIANS 4:13-16 NKJV

That is our goal. To grow up and become more and more like Christ until that time that we are in fact in His midst, perfected forever. We are, for now, still in bodies that are tempted and which sin on occasion. Paul describes the transitory position of one seeking to be mature in Christ: "And I, brethren, could not speak to you as to spiritual people but as to carnal, as to babes in Christ. I fed you with milk and not with solid food; for until now you were not able to receive it, and even now you are still not able; for you are still carnal. For where there are envy, strife, and divisions among you, are you not carnal and behaving like mere men?"

1 CORINTHIANS 3:1-4 NKJV

Is Paul saying that a "carnal" person can not receive "solid food"? What are the characteristics of a carnal person? How does one go about becoming "less carnal".

NOTES/REFLECTIONS

CORE VALUE 30

GOT TOO MUCH STUFF? BUILD A BIGGER BARN!

> **CORE CHRISTIAN VALUE**
>
> What a temptation it is to accumulate wealth, which we know will perish. Better to be one who is a "conduit" using wealth to advance the cause of the Kingdom.

"Then He spoke a parable to them, saying: 'The ground of a certain rich man yielded plentifully. And he thought within himself, saying, 'What shall I do, since I have no room to store my crops?' So he said, 'I will do this: I will pull down my barns and build greater, and there I will store all my crops and my goods. And I will say to my soul,' Soul, you have many goods laid up for many years; take your ease; eat, drink, and be merry.' But God said to him, 'Fool! This night your soul will be required of you; then whose will those things be which you have provided? So is he who lays up treasure for himself, and is not rich toward God." LUKE 12:16-21 NKJV

There is a parable in the Bible that speaks of three men being given unequal amounts to invest. One had 5 talents (money), another had 2 talents and another had 1 talent. The one with 5 earned 5 more and the one with 2 earned 2 more and the one with a single talent hid it and did nothing with it. When the master came he commended the two who had doubled their holdings and scolded the man who hid his single talent. I will say that the lesson is that God intends us to use the talents he has given us and not to hide them away. Therefore, endeavor (hard work) is encouraged and rewarded. That being the case, how can the accumulation of wealth lead to a problem? Listen to the answer:

"Command those who are rich in this present age not to be haughty, nor to trust in uncertain riches but in the living God, who gives us richly all things to enjoy. Let them do good, that they be rich in good works, ready to give, willing to share, storing up for themselves a good foundation for the time to come, that they may lay hold on eternal life." 1 TIMOTHY 6:17-19 NKJV

If God has richly blessed you, do good. Be ready to give, be willing to share, giving God the credit for His blessing to you and for His gifts to you that can be distributed as the Spirit leads. Do not look for ways to hoard the bounty that decays and will not endure. Listen: "Do not lay up for yourselves treasures on earth, where moth and rust destroy and where thieves break in and steal; but lay up for yourselves treasures in heaven, where neither moth nor rust destroys and where thieves do not break in and steal. For where your treasure is, there your heart will be also." MATTHEW 6:19-21 NKJV

God teaches us that riches can become corrupted and moth eaten and that the corrosion of riches will be a witness against you (JAMES 5:1-3). Building bigger barns to house blessings that overflow appears to be a serious error in judgment for God's children. Do you feel that God has "gifted" you in some way, perhaps not monetarily? What do you think God expects you to do with the gifts that He gives you? What do you think it means when it says you should "store up a good foundation for the time to come". How do you "store up" that which you are to give away? Since passing the blessings along, whether monetary or other "talents" seems to be a requirement, why should you bother working hard? What is in it for you?

Since the Bible says, "You have lived on the earth in pleasure and luxury; you have fattened your hearts as in a day of slaughter" (JAMES 5:5) in a critical way, how can you succeed and not fail?

Is the accumulation of assets some kind of a curse if you fail to understand why God has blessed you? Do assets represent a liability, a responsibility? Why should you hope to be financially successful (if you do have such a hope?)

NOTES/REFLECTIONS

CORE VALUE 31

HOW CAN YOU POSSIBLY SPEAK AS JESUS?

> **CORE CHRISTIAN VALUE**
>
> **The power of the Holy Spirit allows you to be a spokesperson beyond any level of skill you could possibly imagine. When empowered, you can say "I live, yet not I, but Christ liveth in me." GALATIANS 2:20 NKJV**

"Nation will rise against nation, and kingdom against kingdom. And there will be great earthquakes in various places, and famines and pestilences; and there will be fearful sights and great signs from heaven. But before all these things, they will lay their hands on you and persecute you, delivering you up to the synagogues and prisons. You will be brought before kings and rulers for My name's sake. But it will turn out for you as an occasion for testimony. Therefore settle it in your hearts not to meditate beforehand on what you will answer; for I will give you a mouth and wisdom which all your adversaries will not be able to contradict or resist." LUKE 21:10-16 NKJV

There is the answer. When your adversaries accuse you, and they will when nation rises against nation, in the end times, do not worry about being able to speak as Jesus for He will give you a mouth and wisdom that exceed your personal abilities. He will, by the power of the Holy Spirit, empower you. Listen to Luke explain it: "…do not worry about how or what you should answer, or what you should say. For the Holy Spirit will teach you in that very hour what you ought to say." LUKE 12:11-12 NKJV

When Moses was called upon by God to lead God's people out of Egypt to the Holy Land, Moses complained to God about his inability to speak well. Listen to God's answer: So the LORD said to him, "Who has made man's mouth? Or who makes the mute, the deaf, the seeing, or the blind? Have not I, the LORD? Now therefore, go, and I will be with your mouth and teach you what you shall say." EXODUS 4:11-12 NKJV. Moses found that it was God who would supply him with words, wisdom and courage.

There was an occasion, just after the gift of the Holy Spirit had been given to the followers of Jesus, that Stephen, who had been appointed to leadership duties, was "full of faith and power". He did great wonders and signs among the people. Then things turned ugly. "...there arose some from what is called the Synagogue of the Freedmen ...disputing with Stephen." And the Bible says, "they were not able to resist the wisdom and the Spirit by which he (Stephen) spoke." ACTS 6:8-10 NKJV

Stephen, who was stoned to death that same hour by those who disagreed with him, gave one of the most moving speeches in the Bible (ACTS Ch. 7) and finished by saying words very similar to those said by Christ on the cross as the enemies of Jesus killed him. "Lord, do not charge them with this sin." Have you the courage to declare your faith in Jesus when surrounded by the enemy? Does the Holy Spirit embolden you? Listen: "...do not worry about how or what you should speak. For it will be given to you in that hour what you should speak; for it is not you who speak, but the Spirit of your Father who speaks in you." MATTHEW 10:19-20 NKJV

Doesn't it seem wrong to worry about the enemies of Christianity coming after you in your present circumstances? Can you envision a time when those who hate Jesus will hate you? What does the Bible tell you about expecting persecution? Where will you get the wisdom to respond? Before you face an enemy, remember your objective. It is in verse 13, below. "Create in me a clean heart, O God, And renew a steadfast spirit within me. Do not cast me away from Your presence, And do not take Your Holy Spirit from me. Restore to me the joy of Your salvation, And uphold me by Your generous Spirit. Then I will teach transgressors Your ways, And sinners shall be converted to You." PSALM 51:10-13 NKJV

NOTES/REFLECTIONS

CORE VALUE 32

ARE TATTOOS A PROBLEM?

> **CORE CHRISTIAN VALUE**
>
> The Scriptures say, "no tattoo marks." The trend towards tattoos seems to be a significant mistake. Your body is the Temple of the Holy Spirit. No intentional scars, no indelible marks.

The Scriptures only mention the word "tattoo" once. Listen: You shall not make any cuttings in your flesh for the dead, nor tattoo any marks on you: I am the LORD. LEVITICUS 19:28 NKJV. In most cases, the Bible places the "cutting of the flesh" in the context of making permanent visible marks on your skin in honor or memory of the dead. You have seen pictures of some cultures that intentionally scar themselves.

Let's approach this issue in a different light. Why would you refrain from making indelible and intentional marks on your body? Here is one possible explanation offered by the apostle Paul: "What? Know ye not that your body is the temple of the Holy Ghost which is in you, which ye have of God, and ye are not your own? For ye are bought with a price: therefore glorify God in your body, and in your spirit, which are God's." 1 CORINTHIANS 6:19-20 NKJV

To stay with that theme, let's listen to further advice from Paul: "I beseech you therefore, brethren, by the mercies of God, that you present your bodies a living sacrifice, holy, acceptable to God, which is your reasonable service. And do not be conformed to this world, but be transformed by the renewing of your mind, that you may prove what is that good and acceptable and perfect will of God." ROMANS 12:1-2 NKJV

Do you feel that at times we are trying too hard to "conform to this world?" What does it mean to "conform"? Is the failure to conform a source of discomfort, of not fitting in? The answer is often yes; it is not fun to not "fit in".

The Scriptures promise that you will feel out of step with the decisions made by non-Christians. "Blessed are you when men hate you, And when they exclude you, And revile you, and cast out your name as evil, For the Son of Man's sake. Rejoice in that day and leap for joy! For indeed your reward is great in heaven…" LUKE 6:22-23 NKJV

The apostle John quotes Jesus and says: "If the world hates you, you know that it hated Me before it hated you. If you were of the world, the world would love its own. Yet because you are not of the world, but I chose you out of the world, therefore the world hates you." JOHN 15:18-19 NKJV. John then says: "Do not marvel, my brethren, if the world hates you." 1 JOHN 3:13 NKJV. And finally Jesus makes the same point in the Gospel of MARK: "And you will be hated by all for My name's sake. But he who endures to the end shall be saved." MARK 13:13 NKJV

"Therefore the world does not know us, because it did not know Him. Beloved, now we are children of God; and it has not yet been revealed what we shall be, but we know that when He is revealed, we shall be like Him, for we shall see Him as He is. And everyone who has this hope in Him purifies himself, just as He is pure." 1 JOHN 3:1-3 NKJV

When you meet Jesus face to face, how do you want to appear? Are your judgments about your appearance, right now, based on what you think that Jesus will say when He meets you? The verses above says, "we shall be like Him" and "He is pure". Jesus is the yardstick by which we must measure our conduct and our appearance. When you feel tough decisions are upon you, fall back on the basic question, "what would Jesus do?" Then seek His counsel and guidance and do what He would do.

NOTES/REFLECTIONS

CORE VALUE 33

ONE VERY BAD MARK, 666, ONE GOOD MARK; CHOOSE!

> **CORE CHRISTIAN VALUE**
>
> **Choosing to be obedient and faithful to God is a right choice, for eternity. If, in the end, you accept the mark of the beast, in order to buy and sell, you lose. It is God's mark you want!**

Three and one half years into the Tribulation Period, after the temple in Jerusalem has been rebuilt and after treaties have been executed with the opponents of Judaism, the anti-Christ will announce that all sacrifices at the temple will cease and the temple will be destroyed. To more fully understand this prophecy please read, The Unmistakable Events which Chronicle the Tribulation (CHAPTER 10 of the "Israel the Chosen or the Enemy?" web site).

When the temple is destroyed, the prince (the anti-Christ) assumes world leadership and insists on subservience from all people. He achieves that through immense persuasive power and logical exhortation (not as a lunatic dressed in a devil's costume). To make sure that all people comply with his leadership, he ordains that every person must receive the "mark of the beast". Again, he won't call it that and he will not appear to be crazy but without the mark, persons cannot "buy and sell". In other words, the mark would function as a scannable imprint, or a chip imbedded under the skin. We have that technology now as implants in animals. Listen to Merriam-Webster's definition and the idea will be made clear: Scannable: to pass an electron beam over and convert (an image) into variations of electrical properties (as voltage) that convey information electronically. When you go to the market that is how the "scanner" works.

Now listen to how the Bible describes the scenario: "He causes all, both small and great, rich and poor, free and slave, to receive a mark on their right hand or on their foreheads, and that no one may buy or sell except one who has the mark or the name of the beast, or the number of his name. Here is wisdom. Let him who has understanding calculate the number of the beast, for it is the number of a man: His number is 666." REVELATION 13:16-18 NKJV

Then, the Bible makes it clear that accepting the mark is a huge mistake: …"If anyone worships the beast and his image, and receives his mark on his forehead or on his hand, he himself shall also drink of the wine of the wrath of God, which is poured out full strength into the cup of His indignation. He shall be tormented with fire and brimstone in the presence of the holy angels and in the presence of the Lamb. And the smoke of their torment ascends forever and ever; and they have no rest day or night, who worship the beast and his image, and whoever receives the mark of his name." REVELATION 14:9-11 NKJV

It will not be a simple matter to say "no" to the mark. Listen to the fate of those who refused and then understand what God has in store for His faithful servants: "And I saw thrones, and they sat on them, and judgment was committed to them. Then I saw the souls of those who had been beheaded for their witness to Jesus and for the word of God, who had not worshiped the beast or his image, and had not received his mark on their foreheads or on their hands. And they lived and reigned with Christ for a thousand years. They shall see His face, and His name shall be on their foreheads." REVELATION 20:3-4, 22:4 NKJV

Since this is an "end times" situation, you may never face the choice of accepting the "mark". But, do you feel you have the imprint of Christ on your heart now? Have you decided not to follow those who are disobedient? Can people "see" the mark of Jesus on your life? How courageous must your love of God and your neighbors be? Can you withstand temptation, of all kinds, on your own?

NOTES/REFLECTIONS

CORE VALUE 34

WHOSE TEAM ARE YOU ON?

> **CORE CHRISTIAN VALUE**
>
> **God has called us all to be on His team. When we choose to follow Satan, it does not come as a surprise to God, but what is a surprise is that God still seeks us! Respond to His love.**

As kids, we often pick teams. Two people are named as "choosers" (captains, if the other kids will let you get away with that title). You end up on the team of the person who chose you. Did you realize that the world's population consists of just two teams? The difference is that the captain of one team chose every single person to be on His team before the other captain (Satan) got his chance to choose. The other captain, Satan, was given the right to try to "recruit" team mates from God's team. Listen:

"Then those who feared the LORD spoke to one another, And the LORD listened and heard them; So a book of remembrance was written before Him For those who fear the LORD And who meditate on His name. 'They shall be Mine,' says the LORD of hosts, 'On the day that I make them My jewels. And I will spare them as a man spares his own son who serves him.' Then you shall again discern Between the righteous and the wicked, between one who serves God And one who does not serve Him." MALACHI 3:16-18 NKJV

I wish, for the sake of children, that it said, "The people were all playing and the Lord listened to them and He could tell who loved Him and He said 'These are mine. I will give trophies to them all and protect them just as their fathers do'" By inference, that conversation also means that God can tell who did not choose to remain on His team but who chose to be with the wicked, not serving God but serving Satan.

How do we know that everyone was chosen by God? Paul instructed young Timothy to pray for all men "…that we may lead a quiet and peaceable life in all godliness and reverence. For this is good and acceptable in the sight of God our Savior, who desires all men to be saved and to come to the knowledge of the truth."

1 TIMOTHY 2:2-4 NKJV

There you have it! God desires all men be saved. In effect, He has asked all men to be on His team. You have to "opt out", or quit the team to join Satan. Does God know who will quit? Yes, He knows, even before we are born, who will love Him and we do not. We never know about the final fate of another person. We see how they live their lives and we guess whose team they are on, but only God knows the final outcome. We are to pray for our enemies and those who do not appear to love God. We should hope that they get on the winning side before the game is over.

Listen to this wonderful PSALM: The LORD is near to all who call upon Him, to all who call upon Him in truth. He will fulfill the desire of those who fear Him; He also will hear their cry and save them. The LORD preserves all who love Him, But all the wicked He will destroy. PSALM 145:18-20 NKJV

Aren't you sorry about those who choose to remain wicked? How can you show them how good it is to love God and be loved by our Lord and Savoir? Is it worth the effort? Is it okay to just let them go? Who is responsible for "winning" a soul over to the Lord's team? Do you see yourself as the captain or the team mate? Is it just too hard to be kind to an unkind person? Where can you turn for strength and courage?

NOTES/REFLECTIONS

CORE VALUE 35

DOES GOD REALLY HEAR MY PRAYERS?

> **CORE CHRISTIAN VALUE**
>
> **God is love and He requires us to love others as He loves us. If we are angry with our brothers we must first forgive them before asking God to forgive us and to hear our prayers.**

Let's begin with the opposite question; to whom does God not listen? The answer is immediately clear. "Now we know that God does not hear sinners" JOHN 9:31 NKJV. Have you ever felt that God does not hear your prayers? We know that God wants us to call upon Him and to seek a personal relationship with Him through Jesus and the communion of the Holy Spirit but we also know that if we are completely out of sync with God that it would be like being angry and uncaring toward a friend and then expecting that friend to care for us. First we have to make things right with our friend and then a good relationship can follow but if we do not ask for forgiveness we should not expect it.

It even gets more clear that God won't listen to us if we are angry and uncaring toward a friend. Listen to Jesus: "But I say to you that whoever is angry with his brother without a cause shall be in danger of the judgment. And whoever says to his brother, 'Raca!' (means a word of utter contempt, signifying "empty," intellectually rather than morally),shall be in danger of the council. But whoever says, 'You fool! (means a godless, moral reprobate).' shall be in danger of hell fire. Therefore if you bring your gift to the altar, and there remember that your brother has something against you, leave your gift there before the altar, and go your way. First be reconciled to your brother, and then come and offer your gift." MATTHEW 5:22-25 NKJV. Here we learn that if we call a friend, a brother, Raca or fool, which are heavy-duty insults, that Jesus says "First, be reconciled with your brother, then come offer your gift." Are gifts of our selves and our resources to God without value if we are angry towards our brothers? That appears to be the case. Listen to the Apostle John:

"If someone says, 'I love God,' and hates his brother, he is a liar; for he who does not love his brother whom he has seen, how can he love God whom he has not seen? And this commandment we have from Him: that he who loves God must love his brother also." 1 JOHN 4:20-21 NKJV. That is a powerful lesson! We must never condemn a brother in one breath and say we love God in the next. Listen:

"Beloved, let us love one another, for love is of God; and everyone who loves is born of God and knows God. He who does not love does not know God, for God is love. In this the love of God was manifested toward us, that God has sent His only begotten Son into the world, that we might live through Him. In this is love, not that we loved God, but that He loved us and sent His Son to be the propitiation for our sins. Beloved, if God so loved us, we also ought to love one another." 1 JOHN 4:7-11 NKJV

There is a wonderful Christian hymn called "love and obey, for there is no other way..." There are two manifestations of your faith in Jesus. They are to love God with all of your heart, mind, soul and strength and to love your neighbor as yourself and to be obedient to God's will for your life. If you want God to listen to your prayers, listen to advice from the Apostle John: "...if anyone is a worshiper of God and does His will, He hears him." JOHN 9:32 NKJV

Do you feel God hears your prayers? What sort of things might get in the way of God hearing your prayers? How hard is it to forgive someone that has not forgiven you? When the Apostle John said, "we must do His will" to be heard does the reverse of that basically say that if we are not doing God's will, He will not hear us? Is it as simple as "love and obey"? How does true love manifest itself?

NOTES/REFLECTIONS

CORE VALUE 36

DID YOU SAY "ASK ANYTHING"?

> **CORE CHRISTIAN VALUE**
>
> We are able to ask our Lord for anything and be sure we will receive it if the thing we ask for is consistent with His will. His will for your life has already been established! Seek His will.

The following verse has raised many questions over the years. Listen: "Now this is the confidence that we have in Him, that if we ask anything according to His will, He hears us. And if we know that He hears us, whatever we ask, we know that we have the petitions that we have asked of Him." 1 JOHN 5:14-15 NKJV

Clearly, if we ask anything "according to His will", then our will and His will are in agreement. We are asking God to do for us that which is His will. We are invited to ask. This is not a circumstance in which being timid or uncertain is advised. Humility and contrition before our Lord and Savior are always necessary conditions for entering into His presence, but having said that, boldness in seeking His will and asking for His assistance in doing His will for our lives is more than okay. Listen to the Apostle Paul:

"(that)...the manifold wisdom of God might be made known by the church to the principalities and powers in the heavenly places, according to the eternal purpose which He accomplished in Christ Jesus our Lord, in whom we have boldness and access with confidence through faith in Him." EPHESIANS 3:10-12 NKJV

Paul says we are to be bold and confident through our faith in Him. It is our faith in Him that permits this boldness, not faith in ourselves, but faith in Jesus who we know loves us. The author of the Book of Hebrews (The author is unnamed but many believe Paul was the author) further clarifies matters.

"Seeing then that we have a great High Priest who has passed through the heavens, Jesus the Son of God, let us hold fast our confession. For we do not have a High Priest who cannot sympathize with our weaknesses, but was in all points tempted as we are, yet without sin. Let us therefore come boldly to the throne of grace, that we may obtain mercy and find grace to help in time of need." HEBREWS 4:14-16 NKJV

The "therefore" in verse 16 above refers to the fact that Jesus, our High Priest, knows what it is like to be tempted with sin. It says Jesus sympathizes with our situation. We are not alone as we face trials and our "needs" are not unknown. We boldly enter into the presence of One who knows us, loves us and who lived without sin in a sinful world. If we pray according to His will for us we can confidently know that His will is going to be done. Thus our prayers should always be, Lord willing, I want this or that to occur. Listen to James, the half brother of Jesus as he gives you excellent perspective:

"Come now, you who say, 'Today or tomorrow we will go to such and such a city, spend a year there, buy and sell, and make a profit'; whereas you do not know what will happen tomorrow. For what is your life? It is even a vapor that appears for a little time and then vanishes away. Instead you ought to say, 'If the Lord wills, we shall live and do this or that.'" JAMES 4:13-15 NKJV

Do you always remember to say "Lord willing" as you start or end your prayers? Do you realize that His will for your life has already been established? Is it His light on our path that we seek? When you pray for others, do you ask for God's will to be done in their lives? What is God's will for all mankind?

NOTES/REFLECTIONS

CORE VALUE 37

GOD HAS NO GRANDCHILDREN.

> **CORE CHRISTIAN VALUE**
>
> **Parents should pray earnestly for the salvation of their children but children grow up and they must each choose to love and obey our Lord. Mature believers stand alone before God.**

Do you ever feel like you are part of God's family because your mom or dad loves the Lord? Is it sort of like mom or dad is the child of God and you are the grandchild? Listen to Paul teaching young Timothy about grandchildren:

"I thank God, whom I serve with a pure conscience, as my forefathers did, as without ceasing I remember you in my prayers night and day, greatly desiring to see you, being mindful of your tears, that I may be filled with joy, when I call to remembrance the genuine faith that is in you, which dwelt first in your grandmother Lois and your mother Eunice, and I am persuaded is in you also."

2 TIMOTHY 1:3-5 NKJV

First, this grandchild is Timothy, a young man that Paul prayed for unceasingly. When a righteous man prays to God it is of great benefit to the target of their prayers. Listen to James: "Confess your trespasses to one another, and pray for one another, that you may be healed. The effective, fervent prayer of a righteous man avails much." JAMES 5:16 NKJV. When we who love the Lord, pray for our children and grandchildren, it makes a difference!

Second, we see that a faithful mother and grandmother had a positive effect on Timothy. But the point upon which we must focus is this; God has no grandchildren. Each of us, as we achieve maturity and are wise enough to know right from wrong, must choose for ourselves to love God. When we are judged as mature persons, we are judged individually, not as a family. Our relationship to our Lord must be personal and individualized. The faith of our family members is a great assist but faith is not something we inherit, it is something we personally acquire by the grace of God, having faith in our Lord, Jesus Christ, and then acting on that faith in our daily lives. Listen as Jesus teaches us about accountability:

"For the Son of Man will come in the glory of His Father with His angels, and then He will reward each according to his works." MATTHEW 16:27 NKJV. We will each be rewarded according to our works, that is, as a person of faith, the actions that you took with the resources God gave you (strength, wisdom, wealth, etc.) will form the basis of your standing before Jesus at the time of judgment. That is why we must not take comfort in the works of our family members; we must develop our own record of service to our Lord. The faith of a family member is of assistance as Paul explains here: "For the unbelieving husband is sanctified by the wife, and the unbelieving wife is sanctified by the husband; otherwise your children would be unclean, but now they are holy." 1 CORINTHIANS 7:14 NKJV.

But still, the child is born "clean" because of a believing mother or father will mature and then this child, born clean, will be rewarded according to that child's faith and obedience.

Does being a member of a Christian organization make you a Christian? If you are a member of a Christian family, and are mature, does that make you a Christian? Does having a Christian as a best friend mean that you are a Christian too? Are younger, not yet accountable children, advantaged by having been raised in a Christian family? Does God love and protect all young children?

NOTES/REFLECTIONS

CORE VALUE 38

BABEL REVERSED; A PURE LANGUAGE RESTORED.

> **CORE CHRISTIAN VALUE**
>
> **When man tried to glorify himself and build the tower of Babel, God confused their language. They no longer spoke a single language. In heaven, God will restore a pure language.**

Do you know the story of the Tower of Babel? Do you wonder where all the multiple languages of the world originated? Listen to the story:

"Now the whole earth had one language and one speech. And it came to pass, as they journeyed from the east, that they found a plain in the land of Shinar, and they dwelt there. Then they said to one another, "Come, let us make bricks and bake them thoroughly." They had brick for stone, and they had asphalt for mortar. And they said, "Come, let us build ourselves a city, and a tower whose top is in the heavens; let us make a name for ourselves, lest we be scattered abroad over the face of the whole earth." But the LORD came down to see the city and the tower which the sons of men had built. And the LORD said, "Indeed the people are one and they all have one language, and this is what they begin to do; now nothing that they propose to do will be withheld from them. Come, let Us go down and there confuse their language, that they may not understand one another's speech." So the LORD scattered them abroad from there over the face of all the earth, and they ceased building the city. Therefore its name is called Babel, because there the LORD confused the language of all the earth; and from there the

LORD scattered them abroad over the face of all the earth." GENESIS 11:1-9 NKJV

When those who love God are together in heaven, how are they going to communicate? Listen: "For then I will restore to the peoples a pure language, That they all may call on the name of the LORD, To serve Him with one accord." ZEPHANIAH 3:9 NKJV. There is the answer. The incident which brought multiple languages to the world's citizens will be reversed. In heaven, we will all speak the same language.

There was an incident after Jesus had been resurrected and had appeared to over 500 persons, where many from foreign lands, who spoke foreign languages, were in Jerusalem celebrating the Passover. Those who had just been filled with the power and gift of the Holy Spirit began to witness to the multitude, but those witnessing spoke in the language of the foreigners. Listen to Luke's account:

"And there were dwelling in Jerusalem Jews, devout men, from every nation under heaven. And when this sound occurred, the multitude came together, and were confused, because everyone heard them speak in his own language. Then they were all amazed and marveled, saying to one another, 'Look, are not all these who speak Galileans? And how is it that we hear, each in our own language in which we were born? Parthians and Medes and Elamites, those dwelling in Mesopotamia, Judea and Cappadocia, Pontus and Asia, Phrygia and Pamphylia, Egypt and the parts of Libya adjoining Cyrene, visitors from Rome, both Jews and proselytes, Cretans and Arabs – we hear them speaking in our own tongues the wonderful works of God.' So they were all amazed and perplexed, saying to one another, 'Whatever could this mean?'" ACTS 2:5-12 NKJV

If God can simply "will" us to begin speaking in a new language and can, by His will, restore us to a pure language, does that help you understand His sovereignty, his omniscience and His power. Heaven will be a place where we all are able to communicate, perfectly. Can you envision the chaos of celebration, if we did not speak a single language? Does this example of God's power clarify his level of control? Is this one more illustration of his concern for our well being? Is it an act of love?

NOTES/REFLECTIONS

CORE VALUE 39

COULD BLESSINGS BECOME BURDENS?

> **CORE CHRISTIAN VALUE**
>
> **Our talents, wealth and gifts are accompanied by this instruction: To whom much is given, much is required. The capacity to love is a gift freely given by God. Spend this resource!**

Have you ever thought about the notion that great gifts create great obligations as well as great opportunities? You have heard or you will hear the following statement about great gifts: To whom much is given, much is required. You could look at that statement in reverse and say "if you don't have much, I guess that not much is required of you". Do you feel you don't have much? Is having "much" always about money, real estate or other tangible assets? No, there are persons whose wealth lies in their heart. They have received the gift of love and they are able to give of it freely.

Would you say that "having a heart to give support, love, and care to others" is a gift? What if you do not exercise the gift? Is it still a gift? Suppose the gift is made freely available to you but you decide to "pass", a sort of no thanks to the offer of "receiving a new heart, one that freely gives love and support to others." There are those who yearn to be righteous, to be like Jesus, but who can't seem to get there. One of those persons was Nicodemus, a Pharisee, who came at night when no one would see him and asked Jesus how He could be doing such marvelous things unless He was from God. In effect, Nicodemus wanted to do the things and have the heart for people that Jesus had. Jesus explained:

"Most assuredly, I say to you, unless one is born again, he cannot see the kingdom of God." Jesus went on to say: "That which is born of the flesh is flesh, and that which is born of the Spirit is spirit. Do not marvel that I said to you, 'You must be born again.'" JOHN 3:3, 6-7 NKJV

The Prophet Ezekiel clarified what it means to be born again, to have a new heart: "…I will put a new spirit within them, and take the stony heart out of their flesh, and give them a heart of flesh, that they may walk in My statutes and keep My judgments and do them; and they shall be My people, and I will be their God. EZEKIEL 11:19-20 NKJV

To be born again is to receive a new heart, one that is capable of love beyond the heart we were born with. Ezekiel goes on to say: "…get yourselves a new heart and a new spirit." EZEKIEL 18:31 NKJV Here we learn that a new heart also means a new spirit, one in which His Spirit and your spirit become as one. King David makes the same point. Listen: "0 Create in me a clean heart, O God, and renew a steadfast spirit within me." PSALM 51:10 NKJV

What gifts has God given you. Do you feel that God has heightened expectations of you because of those gifts? Would you rather not have the gift if the expectations are so high? Where do you feel you can turn for the strength to fully utilize your gifts? Does it seem that a gift not utilized might be taken away? (See MATTHEW 25:14-29)

NOTES/REFLECTIONS

CORE VALUE 40

I HUMBLY DECLARE THAT I OUT RAN ALL OF YOU!

> **CORE CHRISTIAN VALUE**
>
> **We seek praise from men and we offer praise to our children. Praise can distort God's hope for us. He tells us to come to Him with all humility and contrition, not wise in our own eyes.**

We seem to have an inherent need to brag. We are so proud of our accomplishments that we can not wait to tell someone else how well we have done. Let's think about the nature of a child for a moment. Children thrive on praise, don't they? We sometimes, in our zeal to make them feel good about what they have done or who they are, overly praise them. We go "over the top" in our statements to them, generally because we truly love them and are truly proud, but we sometimes try too hard to lift up their spirits, even when they have not done as well as we and they had hoped to do. This is a tendency that God knows we have and in the Scriptures He gives us some perspective on this matter. Listen: "But he who is greatest among you shall be your servant. And whoever exalts himself will be humbled, and he who humbles himself will be exalted." MATTHEW 23:11-12 NKJV

We will never stop lifting up our children in praise. We must also try to teach them the importance of humility. When they do well, our praise should be consistent with reality. It is difficult enough to restrain our praise and especially difficult if the praise is intended to console them. Kids are smart. They do not want "false" praise. They do want your unconditional love, not based on their "winning" but based on your genuine support of their intentions.

We, as adults, still like praise. Everyone likes praise! Is this true? If so, what advice does the Apostle Paul offer us and what should we teach our children. Listen: "For I say, through the grace given to me, to everyone who is among you, not to think of himself more highly than he ought to think, but to think soberly, as God has dealt to each one a measure of faith." ROMANS 12:3 NKJV: James, the brother of Jesus, makes a similar point: "For where envy and self-seeking exist, confusion and every evil thing are there." JAMES 3:16 NKJV Jesus said "…for they loved the praise of men more than the praise of God." JOHN 12:43 NKJV

Solomon summed this point up by saying, "Pride goes before destruction, and a haughty spirit before a fall. Better to be of a humble spirit with the lowly, than to divide the spoil with the proud. Then Solomon compares praising yourself with having eaten too much honey. "It is not good to eat much honey; so to seek one's own glory is not glory." Solomon continues: "Do you see a man wise in his own eyes? There is more hope for a fool than for him." And finally, "Do not be overly righteous, nor be overly wise: Why should you destroy yourself?" PROVERBS 16:18-19, 25:27, 26:12 ECCLESIASTES 7:16 NKJV

Then the prophet Isaiah says, "For thus says the High and Lofty One Who inhabits eternity, whose name is Holy: "I dwell in the high and holy place, with him who has a contrite and humble spirit, to revive the spirit of the humble, And to revive the heart of the contrite ones." ISAIAH 57:15 NKJV

Do you see a time when you will ever stop praising those you love? Not likely, but given what you have just read, what are some biblical guidelines about offering praise? It is one thing to focus on how we should properly praise other people but another thing to see ourselves in the proper light before God. If God does not want us to be "proud of ourselves" then how can we react to praise from other men?

NOTES/REFLECTIONS

CORE VALUE 41

WHO FORGOT TO WATER THE FLOWERS?

> **CORE CHRISTIAN VALUE**
>
> **Thirst is real but quenching one's thirst with water satisfies temporarily. To drink of the living water is to be filled with the righteousness of Jesus. Jesus in us sustains life forever.**

How many times have you forgotten to water some living thing such as flowers or shrubs? The plants, unwatered, go into shock, wither and die. Water is essential to life for all living things including each of us. Have you ever experienced incredible thirst? The Bible uses the picture of thirst to teach us about living water.

A woman of Samaria came to draw water. Jesus said to her, "Give Me a drink." For His disciples had gone away into the city to buy food. Then the woman of Samaria said to Him, "How is it that You, being a Jew, ask a drink from me, a Samaritan woman?" For Jews have no dealings with Samaritans. Jesus answered and said to her, "If you knew the gift of God, and who it is who says to you, 'Give Me a drink,' you would have asked Him, and He would have given you living water." The woman said to Him, "Sir, You have nothing to draw with, and the well is deep. Where then do You get that living water? Are You greater than our father Jacob, who gave us the well, and drank from it himself, as well as his sons and his livestock?" Jesus answered and said to her, "Whoever drinks of this water will thirst again, but whoever drinks of the water that I shall give him will never thirst. But the water that I shall give him will become in him a fountain of water springing up into everlasting life." JOHN 4:7-14 NKJV

First Jesus asked for water to drink and then He explained that if the Samaritan woman knew the gift of God, she would have asked to be filled with living water. What did Jesus mean by "living water"? If the living water from Jesus will cause us to "never thirst again", what must the living water be? Jesus tells us that we shall be filled, permanently, if we hunger and thirst for righteousness. Our thirst is not only for the water that sustains life, temporarily, but for the living water, that sustains life forever. Listen to Jesus: "'I am the bread of life. He who comes to Me shall never hunger, and he who believes in Me shall never thirst.'" "...Blessed are those who hunger and thirst for righteousness, for they shall be filled." JOHN 6:35, MATTHEW 5:6 NKJV

What is it to be "filled with righteousness"? Isaiah explains:

"Therefore with joy you will draw water from the wells of salvation ...The LORD will guide you continually, and satisfy your soul in drought, and strengthen your bones; you shall be like a watered garden, and like a spring of water, whose waters do not fail." ISAIAH 12:3, 58:11 NKJV

Jesus then makes it abundantly clear that He wants to satisfy your thirst for righteousness, forever.

I am the Alpha and the Omega, the Beginning and the End. I will give of the fountain of the water of life freely to him who thirsts. REVELATION 21:6 NKJV

Do you drink, only to find yourself thirsty again? What is the nature of "living water"? Does being filled with living water change things for you? What evidence is there that you are filled with living water?

NOTES/REFLECTIONS

CORE VALUE 42

WHICH IS IT, EARTHLY REWARDS OR ETERNAL REWARDS?

> **CORE CHRISTIAN VALUE**
>
> Christians should never accept jobs or roles in life that separate them from God. It is better to spend a day in His Temple than a thousand elsewhere. Serve Him no matter where you are.

In the verse below, Moses could have remained in the palace of the Pharaoh and been the grandson of the king or he could join his people, the Jews, who were being persecuted. Listen:

"It was by faith that Moses, when he grew up, refused to be treated as the grandson of the king, but chose to share ill-treatment with God's people instead of enjoying the fleeting pleasures of sin. He thought that it was better to suffer for the promised Christ than to own all the treasures of Egypt, for he was looking forward to the great reward that God would give him." HEBREWS 11:24-26 TLB

Do we make choices to pass on living in a situation that is clearly outside the will of God? For instance, if someone offered you a chance to live as the favored and personal servant of a very sinful man and they promised you the best of everything for the rest of your life, would you accept the offer? Discuss what excuses you might have for accepting the offer.

Here is one answer offered by a Psalm writer: A single day spent in your Temple is better than a thousand anywhere else! I would rather be a doorman of the Temple of my God than live in palaces of wickedness.

For Jehovah God is our Light and our Protector. He gives us grace and glory. No good thing will he withhold from those who walk along his paths. PSALM 84:10-11 TLB

The Apostle Paul has the following to say: "… life is worth nothing unless I use it for doing the work assigned me by the Lord Jesus-the work of telling others the Good News about God's mighty kindness and love." ACTS 20:24 TLB

What would you like your life's work to be? What things can you think of to do that would make you happy and still be able to glorify God? Do any of the things you want to do tend to separate you from God and his plan for your life? Is it possible to have the very best job or one of the worst and still be happy? Listen again to Paul's view of difficult circumstances.

"We can rejoice, too, when we run into problems and trials, for we know that they are good for us-they help us learn to be patient. And patience develops strength of character in us and helps us trust God more each time we use it until finally our hope and faith are strong and steady. Then, when that happens, we are able to hold our heads high no matter what happens and know that all is well, for we know how dearly God loves us, and we feel this warm love everywhere within us because God has given us the Holy Spirit to fill our hearts with his love." ROMANS 5:3-5 TLB

Trials will come no matter what place you find yourself. You can be God's beacon of light in the darkness and you can be his loyal and trusted servant in his Temple.

NOTES/REFLECTIONS

CORE VALUE 43

I KNOW AND YOU DON'T!

> **CORE CHRISTIAN VALUE**
>
> It is important to know that the Holy Spirit speaks to each one of us personally. No one can receive "your" message from the Holy Spirit but you. Listen to Jesus!

When it comes to understanding the Bible, how much room is there for honest disagreement? Is there only one answer to all questions? We may wish that there was only one answer to all questions but in fact the Bible places a great deal of emphasis on what the Holy Spirit wants to tell you, personally. Yes there are some black and white questions that always have the same answer for every believer (such as the 10 commandments), but there are times that God wants to have you listen to Him for direction that He may not be giving someone else. The Apostle Peter speaks to this issue very clearly. Listen:

And so we have the prophetic word confirmed, which you do well to heed as a light that shines in a dark place, until the day dawns and the morning star rises in your hearts; knowing this first, that no prophecy of Scripture is of any private interpretation, for prophecy never came by the will of man, but holy men of God spoke as they were moved by the Holy Spirit. 2 PETER 1:19-21 NKJV

Prophecy means pointing to the future, describing what will happen as well as teaching. Peter says that no prophecy, no teaching, is of any private interpretation. The meaning of the Scriptures strikes each of us a little differently because we have different needs and different levels of experience.

The one thing that we who love Jesus have in common is the manifestation (the actual presence) of the Holy Spirit in our hearts. Teaching from the Scriptures will never be contradictory. To the contrary, it all fits together perfectly but if you only have limited understanding, let's say due to your youth, a particular teaching may seem clear enough to you now but over time, as you read the Bible, it will become even clearer. Listen to how Paul teaches Timothy the breadth of Scriptural truth:

All Scripture is given by inspiration of God, and is profitable for doctrine, for reproof, for correction, for instruction in righteousness, that the man of God may be complete, thoroughly equipped for every good work. 2 TIMOTHY 3:16-17 NKJV

As to who is teaching you the meaning of the truth, written on your heart, listen to Jesus: ...for it is not you who speak, but the Spirit of your Father who speaks in you. MATTHEW 10:20 NKJV

Discuss how complex the word "truth" is when you think about what God wants to teach each of us. Do the type of questions to which you need answers change with your level of maturity? Do you feel wisdom comes in one "big dose"? What does it mean when it says the word is a light that shines in a dark place, until the day dawns and the morning star rises in your hearts? Has the light fully illuminated the darkness in every heart regardless of levels of maturity?

NOTES/REFLECTIONS

CORE VALUE 44

UNITY IN JESUS, OUR PRAYER

> **CORE CHRISTIAN VALUE**
>
> **Denominationalism is an unnecessary reality, born of division, not unity. Our Lord prefers we be of one mind, exercising the gift of love towards each other.**

Many churches exist that claim to worship Jesus Christ as the Head of their faith. Why is this so? Does the Bible encourage separate churches with different beliefs? Listen to what the Apostle Paul had to say in his letter to the Philippians:

Therefore if there is any consolation in Christ, if any comfort of love, if any fellowship of the Spirit, if any affection and mercy, fulfill my joy by being like-minded, having the same love, being of one accord, of one mind. PHILIPPIANS 2:1-2 NKJV

The Psalmist makes the same declaration. Behold, how good and how pleasant it is for brethren to dwell together in unity! PSALM 133:1 NKJV

After Jesus was crucified and risen, the early church began to take shape. Here is how the worship service was described by Luke:

So continuing daily with one accord in the temple, and breaking bread from house to house, they ate their food with gladness and simplicity of heart, praising God and having favor with all the people. And the

Lord added to the church daily those who were being saved. ACTS 2:46-47 NKJV

The first churches, after the Christians were forced to separate themselves from the Synagogue, were gatherings in the homes of believers. They worshipped with "one accord" with "simplicity of heart", praising God.

When the Holy Spirit is guiding a body of believers, they will not seek divisions. Divisions grow out of petty hearts where individuals seek to control other individuals. What sort of issues do you think might come up to divide a church? Are some of those issues unimportant in the big picture? If you had to write a Creed, a foundational belief document, what would it need to say?

Listen to Paul's instruction to the Corinthians: For by one Spirit we were all baptized into one body — whether Jews or Greeks, whether slaves or free — and have all been made to drink into one Spirit. For in fact the body is not one member but many. 1 CORINTHIANS 12:13-14 NKJV

Does a church thrive on the differences in talents that lie within the body of believers? What if every church was full of individuals who thought they should be the leader or worse yet, what if every member was unwilling to lead? What sort of tasks need to be completed by a church for it to be an effective church? Does the division of tasks, the identification of roles lead to self centered behavior?

NOTES/REFLECTIONS

CORE VALUE 45

PULL TOGETHER OR BE PULLED APART

> **CORE CHRISTIAN VALUE**
>
> Arrogance and pride are not Christian characteristics. God call us to be humble, willing to give credit where credit is due and to know that all gifts we possess are from Him.

It is a hard lesson for a proud person to learn, but going it alone is not God's way. Why is it hard to learn that lesson? It is probably because we are sinning, sometimes unwittingly, by being proud when humility would have been the better choice. Pride may be one of the most subtle sins we commit. Listen to Paul's advice:

Let nothing be done through selfish ambition or conceit, but in lowliness of mind let each esteem others better than himself. Let each of you look out not only for his own interests, but also for the interests of others. PHILIPPIANS 2:3-4 NKJV

There is an old expression that says, "It is amazing what can be accomplished if you don't care who gets the credit." What is it about us that drives us to "take credit" for an idea or for an accomplishment? Does the answer have anything to do with maturity or does this problem persist throughout life? Does a Christian have less of a problem with this than a non-Christian? Discuss why that may or may not be true.

When God was describing the power of the serpent (Satan) to Job, He said: He is king over all the children of pride." JOB 41:34 NKJV. Are we born with a "default setting" of being proud of ourselves? If so, how can this tendency be overcome? Is giving other people credit for their leadership and contributions a good characteristic?

Solomon spoke often of pride as being a serious problem. Listen: He who is of a proud heart stirs up strife ... When pride comes, then comes shame; but with the humble is wisdom. The fear of the LORD is to hate evil; pride and arrogance and the evil way and the perverse mouth I hate. PROVERBS 28:25, 11:2, 8:13 NKJV

That is pretty strong language. Why would our Lord go to such lengths to warn us about pride? Notice the word arrogance being referred to as the evil way. Perhaps that word gives us more clues as to the real problem with pride. Listen to King David describe an arrogant person:

Whoever secretly slanders his neighbor, him I will destroy; the one who has a haughty look and a proud heart, him I will not endure. PSALM 101:5 NKJV

God spoke through Jeremiah when He said: My soul will weep in secret for your pride; JEREMIAH 13:17 NKJV. Did you ever think that your pride and arrogance might cause God to weep for you? God embraces a person with a humble and contrite heart but He resists the proud.

NOTES/REFLECTIONS

CORE VALUE 46

OVERCOME OR BE OVERCOME

> **CORE CHRISTIAN VALUE**
>
> **To be an overcomer is to, by faith, be a child of God, trusting in Jesus Christ as your personal Savior. All of those who overcome will abide in the Paradise of God, forever.**

When the Scriptures speak of our need to "overcome" what is it we have to overcome? Do we have what it takes to overcome? Listen to the Apostle John explain:

…this is the victory that has overcome the world — our faith. Who is he who overcomes the world, but he who believes that Jesus is the Son of God? 1 JOHN 5:4-5 NKJV

The remainder of this lesson will be direct quotes from the Bible. Discuss each quotation.

"Let everyone who can hear, listen to what the Spirit is saying to the churches: Everyone who is victorious shall eat of the hidden manna, the secret nourishment from heaven; and I will give to each a white stone, and on the stone will be engraved a new name that no one else knows except the one receiving it." REVELATION 2:17 TLB

"To everyone who overcomes-who to the very end keeps on doing things that please me-I will give power over the nations. You will rule them with a rod of iron just as my Father gave me the authority to rule them;

they will be shattered like a pot of clay that is broken into tiny pieces. And I will give you the Morning Star!" REVELATION 2:26-28 TLB

"Everyone who conquers will be clothed in white, and I will not erase his name from the Book of Life, but I will announce before my Father and his angels that he is mine." REVELATION 3:5 TLB

"As for the one who conquers, I will make him a pillar in the temple of my God; he will be secure and will go out no more; and I will write my God's Name on him, and he will be a citizen in the city of my God-the New Jerusalem, coming down from heaven from my God; and he will have my new Name inscribed upon him." REVELATION 3:12 TLB

And He said to me, "It is done! I am the Alpha and the Omega, the Beginning and the End. I will give of the fountain of the water of life freely to him who thirsts. He who overcomes shall inherit all things, and I will be his God and he shall be My son. But the cowardly, unbelieving, abominable, murderers, sexually immoral, sorcerers, idolaters, and all liars shall have their part in the lake which burns with fire and brimstone, which is the second death." REVELATION 21:6-8 NKJV

"These things I have spoken to you, that in Me you may have peace. In the world you will have tribulation; but be of good cheer, I have overcome the world." JOHN 16:33 NKJV

"He who has an ear, let him hear what the Spirit says to the churches. To him who overcomes I will give to eat from the tree of life, which is in the midst of the Paradise of God." "He who has an ear, let him hear what the Spirit says to the churches. He who overcomes shall not be hurt by the second death."' REVELATION 2:7, 2:11 NKJV

NOTES/REFLECTIONS

CORE VALUE 47

TO BE FORGIVEN ENABLES YOU TO FORGIVE

> **CORE CHRISTIAN VALUE**
>
> God gave His only Son as a sacrifice for our sins. God forgives us for our sins and He expects us to forgive others who have disappointed us. We must forgive others in order to receive forgiveness.

Have you ever felt that you could never forgive someone? Did someone do something to you that makes them unforgivable? Discuss when this might have happened.

Now discuss the crucifixion of Jesus. What were the words of Jesus as He was dying on the cross? "Father, forgive them, for they do not know what they do." LUKE 23:34 NKJV. If anyone ever had a right to be angry and unforgiving with people, Jesus did. But what did Jesus teach us about forgiveness? Listen:

Happy are the kind and merciful, for they shall be shown mercy... and forgive us our sins, just as we have forgiven those who have sinned against us. Don't bring us into temptation, but deliver us from the Evil One. Amen.' Your heavenly Father will forgive you if you forgive those who sin against you; but if you refuse to forgive them, he will not forgive you. . MATTHEW 5:7, 6:12-14 TLB

Do you see what Jesus said about refusing to forgive someone? Is there someone you need to go to and to tell them that you forgive them?

Listen to Solomon's advice: Your own soul is nourished when you are kind; it is destroyed when you are cruel. The evil man gets rich for the moment, but the good man's reward lasts forever. PROVERBS 11:17-18 TLB

When you are showing others mercy and forgiveness, it is good for you! When you are cruel it is your own flesh that you are troubling. How kind and patient should you be? Listen to Jesus' answers:

"Sir, how often should I forgive a brother who sins against me? Seven times?" "No!" Jesus replied, "seventy times seven! MATTHEW 18:21-22 TLB

"Try to show as much compassion as your Father does. Never criticize or condemn-or it will all come back on you. Go easy on others; then they will do the same for you." For if you give, you will get! Your gift will return to you in full and overflowing measure, pressed down, shaken together to make room for more, and running over. Whatever measure you use to give-large or small-will be used to measure what is given back to you." LUKE 6:36-38 TLB

The Apostle Paul said: Stop being mean, bad-tempered, and angry. Quarreling, harsh words, and dislike of others should have no place in your lives. Instead, be kind to each other, tenderhearted, forgiving one another, just as God has forgiven you because you belong to Christ. EPHESIANS 4:31-32 TLB

Be gentle and ready to forgive; never hold grudges. Remember, the Lord forgave you, so you must forgive others. COLOSSIANS 3:13 TLB

Now, is there someone you need to forgive? Go with the mercy of Jesus and forgive them, today.

NOTES/REFLECTIONS

CORE VALUE 48

PERFECTED, YET NOT PERFECT

> **CORE CHRISTIAN VALUE**
>
> **A Christian has been perfected due to the grace of God in our lives and our faith in Jesus Christ as our Savior. That does not mean we are perfect. We seek to be like Jesus, we press forward.**

How can someone be perfected and not perfect? When Jesus went to the cross for our sins, and as we have faith in that fact, he made it possible for us to stand in the presence of God, just as if we had never sinned. He covered us with His perfection by the shedding of His blood. We are cleansed and our sins are as separate from us as the east is from the west. Why then, in the process of living our lives, do we continue to sin? It is because we are not perfect. We strive for perfection but it will elude us until we are joined with the Lord in a state of perfection, heaven.

Listen to the apostle Paul, one of God's most blessed followers and one who was chosen to bring God's message to the gentiles:

"Not that I have already attained, or am already perfected; but I press on, that I may lay hold of that for which Christ Jesus has also laid hold of me. Brethren, I do not count myself to have apprehended; but one thing I do, forgetting those things which are behind and reaching forward to those things which are ahead, I press toward the goal for the prize of the upward call of God in Christ Jesus". PHILIPPIANS 3:12-14 NKJV

That is a set of verses that everyone should study carefully. Does Paul claim to be perfect? No, he knows he will be perfected in heaven but he confesses that he has not attained perfection. What does it mean to "have apprehended"? Discuss the possibilities in the context of Paul's words. Does Paul place any value on looking back on his sins? Discuss why he does or does not? When does Paul think that the race is over and that the prize is attained? Discuss how perfection is beyond our grasp during this life? Why is this so?

When Jesus went to the cross he eliminated the need for further sacrifices. The writer of Hebrews explains it this way:

"But this Man, after He had offered one sacrifice for sins forever, sat down at the right hand of God, from that time waiting till His enemies are made His footstool. For by one offering He has perfected forever those who are being sanctified". HEBREWS 10:12-14 NKJV

His single offering of Himself, for our sins, means that those who are being made more and more like Jesus (saints) have been perfected forever. Define sanctification. Give examples of evidence that one is sanctified. Listen to how John, the beloved disciple, defines it: But whoever keeps His word, truly the love of God is perfected in him. 1 JOHN 2:5. NKJV

Listen to John again as he states the critical element inherent in a perfected child of God:

"If we love one another, God abides in us, and His love has been perfected in us. By this we know that we abide in Him, and He in us, because He has given us of His Spirit". 1 JOHN 4:12-13 NKJV

NOTES/REFLECTIONS

CORE VALUE 49

ISN'T BEING "LUKEWARM" BETTER THAN BEING COLD?

> **CORE CHRISTIAN VALUE**
>
> The intensity of our first love, the moment that we first knew that Jesus loves us was a key moment. Is being lukewarm toward Jesus acceptable? Never!

Is it possible that the average Christian thinks of an "evangelical", one who proclaims their faith to others, as a little radical? We know that the Scriptures say that a person should not stand on street corners or in the church or synagogue, praying aloud, in order that they may be seen by men. It appears that Jesus was condemning their motive for witnessing, "so that they could be seen by men". What is your reaction to people who seem to be witnessing in order to bring attention to themselves?

Is there a risk in keeping silent when you should be witnessing of your love for Jesus, either verbally or by your actions? Listen to the words of Jesus on this matter: "He who is not with Me is against Me, and he who does not gather with Me scatters abroad". MATTHEW 12:30, NKJV. Have you ever felt you could be "scattering", that is pushing people away from Jesus by your inaction?

What things could you do that would indicate to Jesus that you are a "gatherer"? The list you are about to make, in writing or otherwise, is a critically important list. Take your time and think carefully about what you, personally, could do. It may be useful to also list the things you could do wrong, not especially sinful things, but things that make you appear to be prideful, "that you can be seen by men".

Let's read a quotation from Jesus: "I know your works, that you are neither cold nor hot. I could wish you were cold or hot. So then, because you are lukewarm, and neither cold nor hot,* I will vomit you out of My mouth". REVELATION 3:15-17, NKJV.

This teaching is extremely blunt. It hits us hard because we see that "drifting along with the crowd, singing the songs in church, doing good things on occasion", all are works, by themselves, that could place us in the lukewarm category. Why would Jesus say these words? Are you able to list things that are good works but which may place you in a "lukewarm" position, especially if you do not get around to doing those things that really matter to Jesus?

What are the things that really matter in our relationship with Jesus? Think about when you first discovered that Jesus loves you and how you felt when you responded positively to His love. Did you, in all humility and contrition (define those words carefully for the family), confess your sins and ask for forgiveness, cleansing and inner strength? Listen to the words of Jesus about how your "first love" for Him, was such an important moment.

"Nevertheless I have this against you, that you have left your first love. Remember therefore from where you have fallen; repent and do the first works, or else I will come to you quickly and remove your lamp stand from its place — unless you repent". REVELATION 2:4-6 NKJV

Our first love and the way we felt when we were first embraced by the love of Jesus, is of great importance.

NOTES/REFLECTIONS

CORE VALUE 50

LAST HERE, FIRST THERE, DISABLED HERE, ENABLED THERE

> **CORE CHRISTIAN VALUE**
>
> **God loves every soul He created, whether we are fast or slow, blind or not blind, lame or not lame, coordinated or not coordinated; we are all equal before God.**

We all are created equal, in terms of our heavenly opportunity and we all have equal access to God, but some people, on earth, seem to have big advantages (strength, good looks, quick on their feet and with the eyesight of an eagle), while others have none of those things. It is a very easy thing to be "first", to have all of the advantages or at least that appears to be the case. But let's examine what the Bible says about those who have the most advantages. Listen to the words of Jesus:

"For everyone to whom much is given, from him much will be required; and to whom much has been committed, of him they will ask the more". LUKE 12:48. NKJV

We could look at this teaching and say, "Boy, I am sure glad I don't have much" believing little is expected of you. Money, fame intelligence, speaking ability, and dexterity are all gifts from God. But re-read the words of Jesus up above; do you think all of those gifts carry no particular obligation? What if you were the person with any or all of those gifts? What would you think that God expects of you?

On the other hand, if someone has very few of the visible gifts, does it seem God lets them off the hook? Are they are able to coast along and do nothing, or very little, that would bring honor to God? Can you think of any person who has none or few or these visible gifts, yet they have shown their love for God and man in a very special way?

Yes, there are people who are severely disadvantaged or handicapped here. But listen to how God sees these people: "…God will wipe away every tear from their eyes; there shall be no more death, nor sorrow, nor crying. There shall be no more pain, for the former things have passed away." REVELATION 7:17. NKJV

The Apostle Paul expressed the same concept when he said: For I consider that the sufferings of this present time are not worthy to be compared with the glory which shall be revealed in us. ROMANS 8:18-19. NKJV

That does not mean that suffering here should seem good. It does mean that God understands and that He has prepared a role for those who are disadvantaged. Listen: "And indeed there are last who will be first, and there are first who will be last.". LUKE 13:30 NKJV. Discuss what it might mean to be first here and last there and vice versa? When could being first here have a bad ending? Listen to Jesus:

"But he who is greatest among you shall be your servant. And whoever exalts himself will be humbled, and he who humbles himself will be exalted". Matthew 23:11-12 NKJV. And… "I will make the lame a remnant and the outcast a strong nation; so the LORD will reign over them in Mount Zion from now on, even forever". MICAH 4:7. NKJV

For more on this topic, go to (CHAPTER 24 of the web site "Israel the Chosen or the Enemy?"), to learn more regarding The Lame, the Deaf and Those Who are "Last" will Emerge as "First".

NOTES/REFLECTIONS

CORE VALUE 51

MY CHURCH IS RIGHT. YOUR CHURCH IS WRONG! RIGHT?

> **CORE CHRISTIAN VALUE**
>
> **Christians may be united or divided but there is only one Body of Believers. There is only one true and living God and only one Holy Word of God.**

How many denominations or religious groups can you name? Make a list, out loud. Having done that, doesn't it seem that there are too many if there is only one true God? What do the Scriptures have to say about who is a member of the Body of Believers worshipping this one true God? Listen: For as the body is one and has many members, but all the members of that one body, being many, are one body, so also is Christ. For by one Spirit we were all baptized into one body — whether Jews or Greeks, whether slaves or free — and have all been made to drink into one Spirit. 1 CORINTHIANS 12:12-14 NKJV

Paul places the Son of God, Jesus, in the middle of this issue. He says we are all one body who are baptized into one body, no matter what our race or economic standing. What is that body? It is the Body of Believers, the Church. What does Paul say about someone who is a true member of the Body of Believers? Does he say they are of a particular denomination or religious group? No, what does he say is the common denominator of all Believers? ...we "have all been made to drink into one Spirit".

The argument then is not whether we disagree about the rituals and traditions of churches, some which have been advanced by men, but that we are all born of the same Spirit, the Spirit of Jesus Christ that abides in the heart of all believers. The yardstick between right and wrong has nothing to do with what people call themselves, it has to do with whether they have declared Jesus as their personal savior, the only One with the power to forgive sins and to present us to the Holy Father, wrapped in the righteousness of Jesus.

As to people who believe they have a corner on the truth, listen to the word of God: "These people draw near to Me with their mouth, and honor me with their lips, But their heart is far from Me. And in vain they worship Me, Teaching as doctrines the commandments of men".' MATTHEW 15:8-9 NKJV

The Bible makes it clear that adding to or subtracting anything from the Bible is a major mistake. Listen: If anyone adds to these things (to the Book of Revelation), God will add to him the plagues that are written in this book; and if anyone takes away from the words of the book of this prophecy, God shall take away his part from the Book of Life, from the holy city, and from the things which are written in this book. REVELATION 22:18-19 NKJV

Discuss which of the denominations that you named are adding the words of man to the Bible or subtracting from the primary teachings of the Bible. Then live a life that is an effective witness of your love for your heavenly Father and for all men.

NOTES/REFLECTIONS

CORE VALUE 52

HEY SAILOR!

> **CORE CHRISTIAN VALUE**
>
> **We are each given certain assets such as beauty, strength, wisdom and compassion. The assets tempt us to feel we are really special. Don't live with a "look at me" attitude.**

Getting someone to notice us, whether male or female, has become a driving force in our society. We tattoo our bodies, pierce our bodies, and change our bodies and strive very hard to be noticed. Of course, some of the striving is healthy, such as the desire to stay physically fit but some of it is "over the top".

The primary question for a Christian is what motivates us. Are we seeking our personal glory or are we trying to live our lives in a manner that brings glory to God, not ourselves. The Bible offers a key insight to the question of why our body exists and what our mission is. Listen:

…do you not know that your body is the temple of the Holy Spirit who is in you, whom you have from God, and you are not your own? For you were bought at a price; therefore glorify God in your body and in your spirit, which are God's. 1 CORINTHIANS 6:19-20 NKJV

Did you ever think of your body as belonging to God, purchased at a price? When you think about that fact, it helps you focus on the responsibility of having our bodies bring honor and glory to God. Our body is the temple of the Holy Spirit. As we move about each day we carry Christ with us into every circumstance.

We are as it says in another verse "the temple of the living God". Do you feel your body is the temple of the living God? When you present yourself to the world each day, do you feel you are presenting a person that brings glory to God? What decisions might you make about your appearance that "would not glorify God"?

The Bible has some harsh words to say to those who appear to be more focused on gaining personal attention than in glorifying God.

Therefore God also gave them up to… the lusts of their hearts, to dishonor their bodies among themselves, who exchanged the truth of God for the lie, and worshiped and served the creature rather than the Creator, who is blessed forever. ROMANS 1:24-25 NKJV

James, the brother of Jesus, put it another way: "The Spirit who dwells in us yearns jealously"? How does God seem to feel if we seek to glorify ourselves? Have you ever thought of God as being jealous? Of what could God be jealous? It is our worship of ourselves, or any other false god, that offends God.

"The one who has a haughty look and a proud heart, Him I will not endure." PSALM 101:5 NKJV

"God resists the proud, but gives grace to the humble." ROMANS 13:13-14 NKJV

"Though the LORD is on high, yet He regards the lowly; but the proud He knows from afar." PSALM 138:6 NKJV

The next time you feel like glorifying yourself, think about what it is that God expects of you.

NOTES/REFLECTIONS

www.ingramcontent.com/pod-product-compliance
Lightning Source LLC
LaVergne TN
LVHW040100080526
838202LV00045B/3716